AN INTRODUCTION TO THE STUDY OF HINDUISM

AN INTRODUCTION TO THE STUDY OF HINDUISM

GURU PROSAD SEN

With a Foreword by

Professor Makhan Jha, Ph.D., D. Litt.
Professor of Anthropology
Ranchi University, Ranchi

GYAN PUBLISHING HOUSE
NEW DELHI-110 002

An Introduction to the Study of Hinduism

Guru Prosad Sen

(Religion, Culture, Indology)

ISBN : 81-212-0498-4

Reprinted in 1995 in India by
Gyan Publishing House
5 Ansari Road
New Delhi 110 002

Originally published in 1893

Printed at Tarun Offset Press, Delhi-110 053

Foreword

Guru Prosad Sen in his book "An Introduction to the Study of Hinduism" (1893) presented some of the salient features of this great tradition in a very befitting manner and still today those aspects of Hinduism are highly relevant. He presented Hinduism in such a manner that removed misconceptions of ages. It showed that Hindus are neither superstitious nor idolators, as the terms were understood by the Christian. This book conclusively proved that Hinduism is the most tolerant of all organisations, and that it is prepared to receive any truth from any sources.

The author was of opinion that Hinduism may assimilate even Christianity or Mohammedanism, if the votarist of these religions conform to its custom. Thus, when Raja Ram Mohan Roy attempted to create a *Brahma Dharma* to oppose the Christians, Guru Prosad Sen suggested that how one will attack a religion which will take anything that is good, and reject any thing that is bad? This makes Hinduism the most progressive and vigorous of all religious faith.

It appears, then, that with the exceptions of the Mohammedans, the Christians and the Parsis all over the inhabitants of Hinduism, whether he be extreme agnostics-like the Nastics and Charbaks, or Polytheist, or Sikhs or Vaishnavs or Shivites or Jains or Buddhist—all are Hindus. Hinduism is elastic and embraces all creeds that seems to be suited to the conditions of those who professed it. In this way it has taken what appears to be worthy of preservation in Buddhism, Jainism, Sikhism, Vashnavism and the monotheism of Kabir, all of which were in the beginning bitterly opposed to Hinduism. The extreme repulsion that one time existed between Hindus and Jain is remembered chiefly in such an old world Brahminical precept as "better be trampled under foot by a mad elephant than enter a Jain temple for protection!" All are now Hindus separated one from other by minor caste's rules but still bound together by a feeling of unity. Having before us this view of the History of Hindu, we are prepared for the assertion that Hinduism is merely for the major portion of the Hindu community chooses to do at any particular time. No one who takes note of signs of the times can fail to be struck in the numberless small modifications that have taken place, during the life of the present generation; in the domestic and social habits of Hindus.

Thus, Hinduism is capable of more important modifications, if those who press reforms and go to work cautiously and with patience.

II

After the publication of Guru Prosad Sen's monograph on Hinduism nearly 100 years ago researches into the various dimensions of Hinduism have brought out many socio-religious facts before the students of religion for their kind information and needful use. As a matter of fact, Indian Tradition acknowledges to main strands in Indian religion—the Vedic or the Nigama and the Tantric, Pauranic or the Agama. There has been interactions between these two. The Vedic tradition is mainly the Aryan tradition and Agama tradition is basically the pre-Aryan tradition. But there has been a final blend of these two sets of ideologies, which differ in their original forms in some very deep or fundamental points. We are, however, not concerned with that at the present moment but what is remarkable is the attitude of the Hindu thinkers through the centuries, after the Vedic period, in trying to fit in these two broad systems together. And the result has been something which is unique in the world, and it feels us with admiration for the comprehensive spirit which was displayed in making new fabric out of the warp and weft of the diverse sects and ideas. The fabric is the fabric of Hinduism, in all its wonderful variety.

India has not disdained to enrich herself with the ideologies of other cults and sects from outside, old Iranians and Greeks and Scythian and other people of Central Asia, who came to India in the past. The relationship between India and China through the centuries did not mean a one way traffic only. India gave many things to China but we are now becoming more and more conscious of the facts that India, also took a number of things from the great civilization of China. So, too, the world of the rude and primitive Hunas and Turks had something to give India. India welcomed to her shores the early Christians and the Jews, who were able to give certain new things to the religious thought of India. The Zorostrian Iranians, after their conquest of their country by the Muslims Arabs, also came to India and became a part of the Indian body politic. So, too, in the case of Islam which has influenced India profoundly during the long centuries of its contact with the country, from the beginning of the eighth century A.D. The more we study the matter closely the greater would appear to be the points of contact between Indian religion and sufistic Islam. Sufism was deeply influenced by the Vedanta in its formative period, but, as a system with its philosophy, its monastic organisation and its devotion exercises through singing and dancing. It also impressed Indian religious life in mediaeval period. It must be said however, that whatever India took from other outside faiths, it completely assimilated it to itself. So all these different melody have brought a great harmony in India, and that harmony can be felt only by men and women who have a corresponding harmony in their own souls. Otherwise, with narrow out-look within, what really is a symphony would appear to be a disorder complex or discordant noises.

The variety of the religious cults within Hinduism, each of which offers its allegiance to the vedas and the upanishads of Indian religion and religious experiences, is quite bewildering. And yet, through these we find a most wonderful display of the oneness of the Human spirit.

Considering this oneness in Indian religion, Madhavacharya, many centuries ago, wrote his very valuable treaties in Sanskrit, *Sarva Darshana-Sangraha*, which was a befitting tribute to the unifying, socio-religious traits of Indian religion.

Hinduism, I feel, in its various remifications derived from a common stock is an exceedingly interesting and instructive subject to pursue. It is not at all a single religion with a creed to which everybody must subscribe. It is rather a federation of different kinds of approach to the *Reality* that is behind life. This is the unique character of Hinduism which must be unfolded either by wider circulation of some of the valuable books like this or by the healthy or constructive discussion or discourses on the various dimensions of Hinduism which will, no doubt, strengthen the national solidarity of India. I hope, this book will serve this purpose to a considerable extent in future.

Department of Anthropology, **MAKHAN JHA**
U.G.C. Centre of Advanced Study,
Ranchi University,
Ranchi.

Contents

THE

STUDY OF HINDUISM.

I.—HINDUISM NOT A RELIGIOUS ORGANIZATION.

THE popular notion regarding Hinduism is that it is a religious organization, and essentially polytheistic in its character, that is, in other words, to be a Hindu and to remain a Hindu, a man must subscribe to certain articles of religious beliefs common to all Hindus, must acknowledge the authority of some books (Vedas and Shastras), and the supremacy of certain interpreters thereof. According to this popular notion, very generally accepted as correct, without examination of the grounds thereof, the Hindu is an idolator, and no one who does not worship the myriads of Hindu gods and goddesses, 33 crores in number, is not, and cannot be, a Hindu. To a superficial observer the Hindu rises from bed, eats and sleeps nay, is born, marries and dies with religious rites, and it would almost be rank heresy to say that Hinduism is not a religious organization. Yet nothing can be more erroneous than the popular notion on the subject. Hinduism is not, and has never been a religious organization. It is a pure social system, insisting in those who are Hindus the observance of certain social forms, and not the profession of particular religious beliefs. It has not even a religious creed or a common set of beliefs, nor has it for its guide a particular book, though popularly the Vedas and Shastras are credited with being the books of the Hindus. So far as religious beliefs are concerned, Hinduism embraces within its fold all phases of belief and even of unbeliefs, from the extreme agnosticism of the Nastics and Charbaks, to the popular polytheistic creed of the believers of the myriads of Hindu gods and goddesses. The Hindu Shastras are, to use a Hindu metaphor, a vast ocean, which so far as religion is concerned, the votary, like the Hindu gods of old, has only to churn, to find the nectar of truth, which is exactly suited to the light that is in him. It is perfectly optional with a Hindu to choose from any one of the different religious creeds with which the Shastras abound; he may choose to have a faith and creed, if he wants a creed, or to do without one. He may be an atheist, a deist, a monotheist, or a polytheist, a believer in the Vedas or Shastras, or a sceptic as regards their authority, and his position as a Hindu cannot be questioned by anybody because of his beliefs or unbeliefs so long as he conforms to social rules. This had been the case with Hinduism in all ages, and has not been brought about by the so-called transition state we are now supposed to live in. Extreme shades of beliefs are, and have always been, met with in the Hindu community, nay, even in every Hindu family. Nothing is more common than to find the deism of the Vedantas, the Vaisnavism of Chaitanya, the Sikhism of Guru Nanuk, the phalic worship of the Shaivas in the same family. The father may be a Vaisnav, the mother a Shaiva or a Shakta, the father's brother a Sikh, and the son a deist. The persecutions of *Praládh* (प्रह्लाद) of the legends, by his father *Hirnakashyapa* (हिरण्यकश्यप), for professing a faith differing from that of the father, makes the father even now the object of just execration of all the Hindus. They are all tolerant of each other's faith. The Hindu never quarrels with religious beliefs, and he never enquires into the religious belief of his neighbours. Believing as he does that *Mukti* मुक्ति, salvation, is certain to the good and virtuous, whatever his creed, he leaves the highest spiritual concerns of a man to the man himself. The *Vijmantra* (विजमन्त्र)* forming the cardinal article of a man's faith, may not even be uttered to one's father and mother. It is a concern of the individual himself, and throughout his life remains a secret between himself and his

* The word or words whispered by the Guru to the noviciate at the time of initiation.

religious teacher (Guru). It is not even necessary for a Hindu to have a Guru (a religious teacher) if he wishes to dispense with one (and outside Bengal the family Guru, as an institution, scarcely exists), and his religious beliefs or even unbeliefs are then matters which concern him alone. It is not necessary that the Hindu should attend a church or a religious congregation, and it is certainly optional with him to attend any church or religious congregation,—church service, in the sense in which it is generally understood amongst Christians or Mahomedans, does not exist amongst the Hindus. Wherever there is worship, the priest worships, but does not lead the worship; believers attend, but do not know or hear the *Mantras* (मन्त्र) that the priest addresses to the object of worship.

The fact that Hinduism is not a religious organization makes it the most tolerant system of all systems in the world, and makes it an essentially progressive system. Changes, transitions, it has always passed through, and evolved out of them something for its own. It takes in and assimilates, it hates to imitate, but it beautifully incorporates and makes new ideas its own by going onward with the impetus generated by these shocks. The earliest known shock of the kind was that imparted by the Buddhists. It was a revolution against the Hinduism of the day, and it brought in new ideas to the spiritual interests of mankind, and the prevailing social system in India.

It made a progress which has not been achieved by any other new religious system in India, but it died out, not as is popularly believed, because of Brahminical persecutions, not because Buddhists were bodily expelled from India by force by a *Shunker Acharjia* (शङ्कराचार्य), but because the Hindu philosophy had then incorporated with it all that it had to learn from the Buddhists, and because at that stage, so far as the social organization was concerned, the Indian Buddhists chose to get themselves re-admitted in the Hindu social system. The same has been the case with Jainism, Sikhism, Vaisnavism, and the Monotheism of Kabir. The Hindus have incorporated within their system such of the ideas as each of these new religious systems had to impart, and as suited themselves to the genius of the Hindu races and the surrounding circumstances of their position (these are important conditions), and finished off their antagonists by calling them *A'pna* (आपना), their own. Take, for instance, the case of Jainism, the oldest of the last mentioned systems. It is essentially un-Hindu. As a religious system it discards the Vedas and Shastras and does not acknowledge the supremacy of the Brahmins. Even now, an orthodox Hindu considers it a sin to visit a temple of *Pareshnáth* (परेशनाथ). The Brahmins at one time taught, when Jainism assumed an uncompromising attitude, "better to be trampled under foot by a mad elephant than to enter a Jain temple for protection," and the

Brahmins of the Hindus still keep themselves aloof from all sorts of social intercourse with the Jain priests. The remnants of the Jains in India are of the Vaisya caste and, as in social matters, the Jains of the day have forgotten, or given up, their hostile and unyielding attitude of the past, and do not object to the Hindu rituals as regards marriage, the Vaisya Jains fully intermarry and otherwise intermix socially with the Vaisyas of Hindu persuasions. Take again the case of the Sikhs. They have been ever deemed by the Hindus as Hindus. Runjit Sinha is taken by all the Hindus to have been the last of the great Hindu princes, and it was currently reported that Dhullip Sinha would be welcome back to India as a Sikh and Hindu. The *animus revertendi* to Hinduism is all that is required of a man originally a Hindu, and for those who did not originally belong to the Hindu stock, all that is required is the observance of the current Hindu rites. We have not to go far in illustration of our position. Not to refer to the Maimon of the Bombay Presidency, whose position oscillates between Mahomedanism and Hinduism, and whose position it was proposed to determine by an Act of the Supreme Legislature, we may mention the various hill tribes who have joined Hinduism almost within the memory of man. We have said that for one who did not originally belong to the Hindu stock, all that is required is the observance of the current Hindu rites. We use the word current studiously. We will show hereafter how the rites themselves change with the changes of time. It is not, again, that the new convert as a rule is relegated to the lower stratum of Hindu society. Instances prevail in which, according to the exigencies of the case, the position that has been assigned to the convert has been very high. Witness, for instance, the position of the *Gyálís*, (गयाली) of Gya, originally Buddhistic priests, the Sakaldipi (Singalese) Brahmins, and the Vaisnava Gosains, some of whom in Bengal belong to the *Vidya* (वैद्य) (medical) caste. Its power of assimilation, physical and moral, gives Hinduism a lease of life which has been the wonder of the world in the past, and which will be its wonder for all time to come, unless it correctly understands the Hindu system. That system is essentially an eclectic system, so far as religious beliefs are concerned, and, as we intend to show in a subsequent part of this discussion, in all social matters also. The instances cited above illustrate, we hope, in a marked degree, the position with which we set out, that Hinduism is not a religious organization. The Jains, Sikhs, Vaisnavas, Kaberpanthis, are, to all intents and purposes, Hindus, though the religious creed of each and all, specially that of the Jains and Sikhs, are essentially un-Vedic in origin, and the professors of these religions, though recognised by the other Hindus, as Hindus, do not believe in the authority of the Vedas and Shastras, do not worship the Hindu gods and goddesses, nor acknowledge the supremacy of the Brahmins. If, then, Hinduism is not a religious organization, and the Hindu has the option of choosing for his faith anything from the extreme point of unbelief to belief in a myriad of gods and goddesses, discarding Vedas, Shastras and Brahminical supremacy, what then is it? We will answer the question in the next part of the article.

II.—WHAT IS HINDUISM?

What is Hinduism? The reply is, that what the Hindus or the major portion of them in a Hindu community do is Hinduism. This may appear to be a truism, it is a truism however, the truth of which ought to be enforced. People, both within and without, discuss the subject as if Hinduism was locked up in some sacred books. The Vedas, the Shastras, the Smrities are regarded as books furnishing guides for the conduct of a Hindu's life, and researches are made in the Vedas and Shastras to understand what Hinduism is. Yet it is a fact, and a fact which cannot be gainsaid, that the Hinduism of the Vedas, nay, of the Shastras, is not the Hinduism of the present day. To even the most superficial reader of the Vedas and Shastras it will appear that changes in almost all the departments of the Hindu's life have been going on from age to age. It is not the scope of this paper to enumerate all these changes, but simply, for the illustration of the definition of Hinduism given above, to indicate that such changes have taken place and even now are taking place. What the Hindus in a Hindu community did, when recorded, became the Vedas of old ; what they did at a later age became, when recorded, the Hinduism of the Shastras, and the Shastras that will record the changes of the present day, when those changes we see around us are accepted as accomplished facts, will be the Hinduism of the day. The *Shastrakar* (complier of the Shastras) of our future, will perhaps, when justifying the departure from the Shastras of the mediæval ages, and from practices then only existing in the memory of man, appeal to some text of the Veda or of Manu, as a sanction for such departure, perhaps twist the grammatical construction, and interpret a synonym in the light of his own views. Like *Jimut-Váhana* (जिमुद वाह्न), of old and revered memory, he will possibly disclaim all opposing views as monstrous and un-Hindu. In this, as we suppose in all social systems, practice precedes theories and codes, and practice is accepted as an accomplished fact when it is carried on by the majority, and very shortly after as part and parcel of the system when it becomes the universal practice. We shall illustrate this by giving a few instances within our own memory. Thirty years ago a Hindu of Bengal (perhaps, of Calcutta excepted) would not be a Hindu, if he were to use onions as a condiment to his dishes, or to take a loaf, or a piece of biscuit ; now onions, loaves, and biscuits are no longer prohibited articles of food in many parts of Bengal. Butchered meat is another instance of departure. No one now regards the practice of taking butchered meat as un-Hindu, though many people in Bengal yet scruple to use meat from a butcher's stall. The use of butcher's meat has never been considered un-Hindu in Behar and the other Provinces. Fowls and chickens may yet be regarded as prohibited articles of food in Bengal, but the strong minority who now enjoy dishes of fowl cutlets, soups, roasts, and curries are gaining ground, and will soon become the strong majority, and fowls and chickens will ten years hence, if not in five, come to be Hindu articles of food in Bengal. The Bengali Shastrakar will not have much difficulty in justifying the departure here, as fowls and chickens are not prohibited articles of food in that country of the Hindus, the Maharastra. The caste system even now overlooks taking food cooked by people of an inferior caste, or with them, or even with Mlechas, or Mahommedans. So you can do several things now admittedly un-Hindu without let or hindrance, so long as you do not obtrude your un-Hindu practices ostentatiously to the notice of the community you live in. Changes are thus daily growing, and when the changes suit the genius of the people, they take root and become parts and parcels of Hinduism. This is not simply in matters of articles of food, but in everything around us. Only the stereotyped character, which for good or evil, the Smrities, or that portion of it which is known as the Hindu law in our Courts, has received, by the advent of British government in this country, is calculated to maintain it where it was. The changes in the Smrities themselves, a complete record of which can be easily marked in the controversial portion of the learned codes of Hindu laws, serve to illustrate the position taken above to a very great extent. Take for instance the change, the reform under which the Brahmins came to be subjected to the jurisdiction of the King's Courts, or the Ilbert Reform in the laws of Ancient India. The text of Goutoma provided that "the king is superior to all except Brahmins." The Mitakshara says, that "from the text of Goutoma it must not be inferred that Brahmins are exempted from amercement, for the text is intended for the purpose of generally extolling the Brahminical tribe." It is ordained in the Sutras, 'six things are to be avoided by the King" (acting with respect to Brahmins), "the punishment of flagellation, of imprisonment, of amercement, of banishment, of reprimand, and of expulsion." The author of Mitakshara naïvely says: "The mere order of priesthood is not sufficient to exempt. That the Brahmins in the text mean persons eminently learned, skilled in worldly affairs, in the Vedas and Vedangas, intuitively wise, well stored with tradition and historical wisdom, continually revolving these subjects in their mind, conforming to them in practice, instructed in the forty-eight ceremonies, devoted to the observance of three-fold and six-fold duties, and versed in legal usages and established rules," or, in other words, such persons from whom the commission of an offence or wrong, or the infraction of a right was impossible. Thus, between the age of Goutoma and that of Vijaneshwara, a great change, affecting the privileges of a special class, must have been slowly and gradually effected, and the Hinduism which Goutoma observed and recorded as rules for the guidance of Hindu kings, as regards Brahminical privileges, was not the Hinduism which Vijaneshwara found extant in his days and justified in his learned disquisition.

Another reform in the Hindu law effected during that period, traces of which are clearly discernible in the disquisition of Vijaneshwara, was almost in the same direction—the encroachment on Brahminical privileges as it existed of old. The ancient doctrine was that the *Sabhásadas* सभासद (assessors or jurors) of the King's Court were to be Brahmins. The text was—"a king who investigates, together with the chief judge, ministers, domestic priests *and* assessors at the Court, according to laws, shall attain paradise." Another text enjoined that the persons appointed as assessors or Jurors (*Sabhásadas*), "were to be versed in literature, (*i.e.*,) in the study of philosophy, grammar, &c., and in comprehending the Vedas, acquainted with the laws, (*i. e.*,) familiar with the sacred code of laws, addicted to truth *i. e.*, prone to habitual veracity, impartial towards friends and foes, that is divested of enmity, affection, partiality and prejudice." The earlier commentator, Catyana, reads the text "persons versed in literature, &c," as setting forth the qualification of persons to be confined to the Brahminical tribe; but the author of Mitakshara, commenting on the first of these texts remarks, that the use of the conjunction, 'and,' between the words 'priests' and 'assessors,' evidently propounds a distinction between Brahmins, (priests) and assessors. The author, as an additional argument for the interpretation he adopts, says, that, "for the sake of adding popular confidence to the assembly (King's Council) some persons of the commercial class should also be called in to assist." But the most important change in this direction was with reference to the appointment of Chief Judge (Pradvivak). The text expressly enjoined the appointment of a Brahmin. It says, "A Brahmin acquainted with all duties should be appointed and associated with the assessors, by a king who is unable, through want of leisure, to investigate judicial proceedings;" the author of Mitakshara observes that, "if such a Brahmin cannot be found, the king may appoint a *Kshatrya* (क्षत्रिय), or *Vaisya* (वैश्य)." It is singular how a turn in the grammatical construction of a text, which, however, was deemed sacred and unalterable, did duty for a change in law, but no grammarian ever thought of giving this turn, until he saw that the changed interpretation was necessitated by the changes which he saw all around. Between the age of Catyana and the age of Vijaneshwara, the author of Mitakshara, said to have been the contemporary of Sankara Acharjia, who is generally credited with the expulsion of Buddhists from India, several centuries had elapsed, and India had witnessed a stupendous revolution, and the Hinduism of the day of Catyana, not in this respect alone, for which we have proofs, but in several other respects, for which the proofs and records are not so clear, was not the Hinduism of the date of Mitakshara. We will see how the changes were brought about. There were no Legislative Councils in Ancient India, and no one in authority who could make or unmake laws. The current theory that Brahmins were lawgivers of the land, does not find any support from the record of the Hindu laws. Even the authors of the codes appeal to the past, and the text writers of the past, for the sanction of what they do enjoin. Their only authority is derived from the correctness with which they interpret the present in the light of the past. Anything that would not accord with the existing facts would, we suppose, carry as much weight with Hindus of their days as the *Nava Sanhita* of the late Babu Keshub Chandra Sen does with the Hindus of the present day. The growth of Hindu laws was something like the growth of the Common Laws in England, with this difference, that the Hindu laws did comprise a greater variety of subjects affecting the ordinary daily life of a Hindu than the Common Laws of England did with respect to Englishmen. Both have their origin in the growth of usages, their recognition in courts of law, or, as in the case of Hindus, in the assemblies of tribes, and their final codification by learned men; but, as in India, the codifiers (at least the authors of extant treatises) happened to be Brahmins, it is generally assumed that Brahmins were the legislators of the land. Hindu laws, therefore, are Hindu usages codified. Usages again originated in the doings of the Hindus, and when a new usage sprung up to take the place of the old, we may be sure that at the start some one had the boldness to break through the barrier of an established usage, and was branded as the breaker of the laws until the change he adopted, or sought to introduce, was generally accepted, and it took the place of the established usage. Take, for instance, again, the changes that took place between the age of Vijaneshwara and the age of Jimut Vahana. In Bengal, the joint family system had received a rude shock; and it was no longer the patriarchal system of old that prevailed, but the first splitting of families into individual units. Jimut Vahana in his time finds the change accomplished, and establishes the changes as laws, by refuting Mitakshara, and appealing to the past and the text writers of the past; and as an additional argument, establishes the doctrine of *factum valet*. This doctrine of *factum valet* prevails throughout India; if not in what are ordinarily called the schools of law, but in every other department of a Hindu's life. The flexibility of this beautiful doctrine enables the Hindu to alter his manners, his customs, his laws, nay, even his religion, to the altered spirit of the age in which he lives. Their surroundings, their education, their circumstances, the infusion of new ideas have always influenced the doings of the Hindus, and the Hinduism of every period. The Bengal Brahmins, even of the age of Ballal Sen, appear to have been as unlike their original stock at Kanouj, as Mr. Bannerji returned from England is from the ordinary Bengali Brahmins of the present date, yet the Kanouj Brahmins never question the Brahminical rank of their caste-men in Bengal: both are Hindus, but the Hinduism of the Kanouj Brahmins is not the Hinduism of the Brahmins of Bengal; and this brings us to our definition of Hinduism once again.

This definition, which we have tried to show accords with established facts in Hindu laws, is that *what the Hindus, or the major portion of them in a Hindu community do, is Hinduism.* A few words of explanation seem necessary. It is not Hinduism now to go to England, because the few Hindus who go to England are kept out of caste; but supposing in a Hindu community, the Hindus could go to England without losing caste, or supposing even that a strong majority of that community would allow a Hindu who had been to England to be again admitted into caste, going to England would be no longer an *un*-Hindu practice, so far as that community is concerned. A Hindu, whatever may be the transgressions from Hindu manners he may be guilty of, remains a Hindu so long as he does not lose caste. If he has a *dal* (party) in the community he lives in, he is a Hindu to all intents and purposes. This community is not the whole body of Hindus, nor all the people of his caste, but a small village circle of people consisting, amongst the higher classes, of Brahmins Vaidyas and Kayesthas in Bengal. This small circle, which usually consists of 300 or 400 families interspersed in two or three neighbouring villages, is called a *Somaj*, and the people *Somajiks*. In marriages and *shraddhs*, for those who can afford it, these are the guests who have to be entertained. If in case of any transgressions from caste rules, the *Somajiks* do not find any fault with the transgressor, the latter does not lose caste ; if some of the *Somajiks* have their scruples, but others have not, they divide themselves into parties called *dals* or *daló-dalis*. Nothing is commoner than to find in many villages in Bengal, the *Somajiks* split into different factions (*dals*) over a transgression from an established usage of which some one in the *Somaj* had been guilty, until the question is finally decided by numbers. If the *dal* of the breaker of the established usage is strong, the change is as good as accomplished, the contending factions uniting again in time. There are in the same *Somaj*, or in the same body of *Somaj*-

iks, nay, even in the same families, men of different views—Conservatives, Liberals and Radicals. The two latter at the present day are the product of English education and the onward influences around. Toleration is the order of the day, and the Conservatives, however they may lament the good old days, cannot help being tolerant, because of the prevalence of liberal ideas, even amongst the younger generation of their own families, or because, as in many cases, when education has made progress, and placed the Liberals in any number in commanding positions, they have to give way to the inevitable.

Much shrewdness, intelligence and tact are required of a leader of a *dal* and as reformations, to permeate the masses, must begin here, in these units of Hindu communities, a practical reformer can safely carry out many desired reforms by correctly feeling the pulse of his *Somajiks*. The wise politicians feel the pulse of the nation, the social reformer in Bengal, if he is practical, should feel the pulse of the *Somajiks*. Many reformers in India have spoiled the cause they advocated, by striving to carry out reforms for which the *Somajiks* were not prepared; by, in fact, giving too much speed to their Radical coach. Many a reformer—and in India reformers are *not* reformers, if they are not religious reformers,—has unfortunately marred the cause of reform by treating social reforms as if they were religious reforms. The popular notion is that Hinduism is a complex system, where social usages cannot be separated from religious beliefs. Our reformers cannot rise above this popular notion. They would not separate the domain of beliefs in the supernatural and metaphysical from the every-day common life of man. To them social reforms are not questions of expediency, but cases of conscience. It would be a sin, they say, if knowing early marriages to be mischievous, or, as they call it, wrong, you were to get your children married at an early age. It would be rank hypocrisy, they say, if believing in the equality of men, and knowing that the caste system as it prevails, is not the right thing in all its phases, you were still to be within the pale of caste and not to give it a kick. It would be the height of dissimulation, they say, if not believing or caring for the 33 crores of Hindu gods and goddesses, you were still to pass off as a Hindu. Your life would be a life of contradictions, they say, if while dining on fowl cutlets and mutton chops of an evening, you should sit to supper with your caste-men at *Pungti Bhojan* (पंक्ति भोजद) at night. The Liberal Indian pleads 'guilty' to no such charge. In social matters, he believes that what is expedient is right. It would not be right or expedient in his opinion to wage a hopeless war. It would not be expedient to thrust reforms all at once into the old Hindu systems. The wholesale reform of the Brahmo Somaj is too much for the Hindus, and the result has been that the Brahmos have to form themselves into a separate community. If these earnest workers had but contented themselves to work from within, instead of spending their earnestness in uselessly trying to demolish the citadel of prejudices from without, what further changes might not have come on by this time.

The true Liberal Indian on the contrary would, for good or evil, stick to the Hindu system and fight out the cause of reform from within. He knows, or tries to know, how far education has prepared his *Somajiks* for a desired reform; how far the onward influences have been acting on them, and tentatively introduces, or tries to introduce it in the community in which he lives. There is a struggle nevertheless, but it is the fight of parties, the *dalá-dali* (दलादली) of the *Somajiks*, and not a fight where the reformer has to go out of the field, fearless and undaunted, no doubt, but nevertheless without achieving a victory. To the cautious general the victory is certain. The educated natives are now, in many parts of the country, the leaders of the *Somajiks*, and the spread of education gives them a larger and larger share of influence year by year. They are not true to their colors if, knowing or believing that the country is prepared for a reform, they do not give an onward pull. They have no need for preaching and for preachers. Their only agency is the educational movement in the country. The reforms thus introduced are introduced with the concensus of the people. They take root and permeate the social fabric as a whole, and very soon become part and parcel of the Hinduism of the time. In the next paper we will examine what reforms have been already introduced, and what further progress in these directions is possible.

III.—WHO ARE THE HINDUS?

We have shown, and we hope we have succeeded in proving almost to demonstration, *that Hinduism is what the Hindus, or the major portion of the people in a Hindu community, do;* or, in other words, that Hinduism is not locked up in a book, believed to have been revealed, and does not consist of a set of religious beliefs, but is composed of certain usages and customs, which have always been changing and variable, and that the usages and customs prevalent in a Hindu community at a particular date have formed the Hinduism of that date. But the question remains—who are the Hindus? The particular congeries of usages and customs called Hinduism in the Madras Presidency may not be the Hinduism of Bengal. They differ essentially, yet both are Hinduism, and recognised as such, because they form the usages adopted by the particular Hindu community of these parts; and though, therefore, there need be no universality in what is known as Hinduism in its unessential parts, it follows that there is something universal throughout India, which distinguishes a

Hindu from a non-Hindu, and which, being distinguished from changing and vanishing usages, remains alone, as the unchanging basis in our ideas of *Hinduism* and *Hindu;* we shall thus get at the essential characteristic which will help us in defining the generic name. We have not in our last two chapters clearly defined the essential characteristics involved in our idea of the word *Hindu*, though we have sufficiently indicated what it is.

To ascertain who are the Hindus of this or any other time, it is not necessary for us to go to the past, or to refer to the Vedas, Shastras or Puranas; though a reference to the past might be of some help to test the correctness of the meaning of the term, when we have determined it by a reference to facts and ideas of the present day.

Now, so far as the term is understood at present, it embraces all those people, settled or domiciled in Hindustan, who are neither Christians, Mahomedans, nor Parsis. We have shown that the Jains in India are no longer considered non-Hindus; and the few Buddhists to be found in the monastic orders of India are respected by Hindus as Hindu ascetics. Perhaps even this definition to which we come by negation, as applicable to the Hindus of the present day, might not suit a few years hence, when a settled domicile in Hindustan may not be regarded as an essential idea in the interpretation of the term, and when possibly Hindus will remain Hindus even when they have settled outside India, as they certainly even now continue to be, though migrating to Burmah, or to any one of the islands of the Pacific ocean. Broadly speaking, however, the negative idea stands good for the present. But when we say that all people domiciled in India, who are not Christians, Musulmans, or Parsis, are Hindus, do we mean that there is anything in their religious beliefs which would exclude these people from those from whom they are thus distinguished? We say no. Suppose a Hindu were to believe in the revelation of the Bible, the doctrine of the Trinity, that of original sin and eternal damnation, the atonement and salvation through faith in a Saviour, he would be a Christian, but would not cease to be a Hindu, so long as he continued to be a member of the Hindu caste to which he belongs. So he would be a Musulman by simply believing in the *kulma* (words) "God is Great, and Mahomet is his prophet;" but he would not cease to be a Hindu as long as he was not thrown out of the pale of caste.

Here, then, is the essential characteristic which distinguishes the Hindu from the non-Hindu races of India. All people who are known as Hindus are divided into castes, and there are no people incorporated with the Hindu system, who do not belong to some caste or other. The Hindu system is therefore a hierarchy of caste, and those who belong to this hierarchy of caste are Hindus.

What is this caste? We discover what it is at the present date by reference to the caste requirements: (1) A Hindu belonging to any one caste must not partake of certain kinds of food cooked by any one else but a member of his caste, or sometimes one of a superior caste. (2) A Hindu must not marry outside his own caste. (3) A Hindu must admit that he belongs to stratum so and so, whilst in the highest stratum are the Brahmins. (4) A Hindu must abide by the rules of his caste, as to the marriageable age of girls, as to widow re-marriage and going to sea, and as to prohibited food.

These requirements may be considered as almost general, though there have been exceptions prevalent from the olden times, which exceptions, the careful reader of the Hindu system will notice, were already there before the action of the progressive tendencies of the present age. Thus, for instance, as regards (1):—The Sikhs, who are now incorporated with the Hindu system, must partake of the *Amrit* —अमृत—when presented to one of the chief Durbars, whoever may present it, and with all sorts of people, irrespective of caste (the religion in its days of purity, having been a negation of caste, and the springing up of a Hindu brotherhood in its absence). The Chaitanya Vaisnavas, who, in the vigor of their early growth, rebelled against caste, have still their *Mahatsabs*, (महोत्सव) great festivals, when a Brahmin may not with any decency refuse to partake of food cooked by a Byragi, whatever may have been the caste to which he originally belonged, or touched by any other Vaisnava, whatever his caste. At the Juggernath Khetra (Puri), food (rice, *dál*, vegetable curries, and the rest), after it has been presented as offerings, is sold at open stalls, and it does not matter who touches it, or who sells it. The sensualism of the *Tantras* disdains caste, and caste rules amongst the *tantrics* (तान्त्रिक), followers of the *Tantras*, are allowed to be so far relaxed that the *Bhairabi-chakra* (भैरवीचक्र), an assembly of elites, who admit into their number people of all castes, who eat and drink without any restriction.

As regards (2):—we have a notable exception in some of the districts of Eastern Bengal, where Vaidyas, Kayesthas and Shahus (Vaisyas or Sunris) intermarry. It is curious that such marriages are not * *Anulom* (अनुलोम) in form, as they ought to have been if they were the relics of ancient Hindu custom still subsisting in these parts of the country, but are always *Pritilom* (प्रतिलोम), and as such, must have sprung up as an innovation in later times. They are of the sort which Akbar found it not difficult to introduce in his day, between the royal family of Delhi and the Rajput chiefs. The bride came from the Rajput family into the harem of the Mughal, but a Rajput bridegroom never

* *Anulom* marriage, is marriage of a man of superior caste with a woman of inferior caste; *Pritilom* marriage is the reverse.

took a Mahomedan wife; so a Vaidya girl bride goes to a Kayestha or Sunri house, but a girl of these latter castes is not espoused by a Vaidya, These marriages are distinctly against the rule of intermarriages permitted by the Shastras, but nevertheless, they are considered fully valid and binding, and are even looked upon with approbation, and the offspring of such narriages have all the rights of the offspring of marriages in the same caste. The rule appears to have been reversed for the simple reason that a girl gone out of the family does not affect the family, if she no longer enter the kitchen, and her father's family have not to take food touched by her, a matter considerably easier than for a Hindu to have a wife, and children by such wife, food cooked or touched by whom he would not be permitted to take. The contrary would be the case in taking for wife a woman of a superior caste, for in this case the husband or his kinsman could have no objection to take food cooked or touched by her. Thus, in this instance, the requirement No. 1 has, by its greater rigidity at the present date, or rather at the date when relaxation came to be introduced in requirement No. 2, affected the rule of the Shastras, and brought on an innovation the like of which could not be justified by reference to any text.

As regards (3):—Relaxation has sprung up from time to time, though the Brahmins have, as a rule, generally held their own. A notable instance of this relaxation is the supremacy which the Gyali Pundas, though not Brahmins, have always maintained over the Brahmins, and the priestly authority which the Srikonda (श्रीखण्ड) Gossains (गोसाञि) of the Vaisnava sect in Lower Bengal, belonging to the medical caste (Vaidyas), have exercised over their Brahmin disciples.

As regards (4):—There is a greater degree of variableness here than in the case of the other three rules amongst different races in India in different parts of the country, and no common ground can be traced except that each community has its own rules on the subject, and these rules are often so rigid in their application for the present, that the slightest infringements have resulted in forfeiture of caste. We shall notice the exceptions with the rules.

Before noticing the differences prevailing in different parts of India in all these four-fold aspects of caste, to some extent the result of changes within recent times; the causes that have induced these changes; where further changes are possible and should be allowed to grow; and when the changes should cease; it may not be quite out of place to examine the historical development of caste as an institution in India in the light of the accepted results of researches made by scholars.

Mr. R. C. Dutt, in his admirable work on "*The*

Civilization of Ancient India," proceeds on these data to lay down that there was no caste in the Vedic period, dating from 2000 B. C. to 1400 B. C; that caste, as an institution in India, began to grow in the latter end of the Epic Period, dating from 1400 B. C. to 1000 B. C., with the growth of the influence of priesthood, and the splendour of the royal courts; that it attained a further development in the period dating from 1000 B. C. to 242 B. C.; that it suffered from a revolution during the Buddhist Period, dating from 242 B. C. to 500 A. D., and that it assumed its present rigidity of form during the fifth or Puranic Epoch, dating from 500 A. D. to 1194 A. D.

From the rules of caste as laid down in the *Sanhitas* we find—

1st.—Monopoly of learning by *dwijas* (द्विज, *twice-born*) especially the Brahmins.

2nd.—Increase of ceremonials; the Brahmins alone officiating at the ceremonies, and the assertion and maintenance of the supremacy of Brahmins.

3rd.—Allotment and division of work among the different castes.

4th.—Touch, contamination, and *Priaschit,* (*penances*).

5th.—Interdict of marriages in certain ways.

6th.—The lowest position of the Sudras.

Now compare the above with modern caste, as prevalent throughout India at the present date. (1):—It will be seen that though, as we shall show subsequently, the Brahmins still maintain their superiority as regards learning, the monopoly now nowhere exists. (2):—The ceremonials have been limited within rational bounds, and though the Brahmins even now officiate at them, the Brahminical supremacy no longer exists in any very offensive form, and, as we shall show later on, it has been materially affected by the iconoclastic influences of the age. (3):—The same tendencies are silently affecting the rigidity of the rule under which each caste was separately attached to its work. (4):—The rules on the subject, unless it be with respect to matters of food, are now, excepting to some extent in the Madras Presidency, more honoured in the breach than in the observance. (5):—There has been a greater rigidity growing in the interdict of marriages. (6):—The position of the Sudras has greatly improved and is daily improving.

We shall next explain generally the causes of the differences existing in the four-fold aspect of caste, of the present day, *i. e.*, the four requirements noted above, in different parts of the country.

Now, nothing is more common, as we have shown previously, than a divergence of customs in different parts of India, or even in different Hindu communities living in the same parts of the country. What is considered a Hindu custom in one part of the country, is considered wholly un-Hindu in another. It is hard to conceive when there could have been uniformity amidst these divergencies; when it could have been that *Manava Shastras* (Institutes of Manu) used to guide the Hindus in every part of India in all the rules of life. Whatever uniformity might have at one time existed, when the original Aryans had not yet crossed the Sutlege, it must have given place to divergencies when the Aryans began to settle in different parts of India, and consciously or unconsciously to imbibe the manners and customs of the people amongst whom they settled, and accommodated themselves to climatic influences and their physical surroundings. The same process which Indianised Europeans in days anterior to the present must have greatly modified the Aryanism of the ancient Aryans; and the Hindu system, as we have seen in the previous part of this article, has been always more eclectic, and favourable for the adoption and incorporation of changes, than European systems have been. Then, the aboriginal races, when they became Hinduised, must have retained many of their ancient customs and usages. This accounts for divergencies; but not for all that we mark in different parts of India. Some of the divergencies have arisen quite within historical times, owing to influences which can be distinctly traced, as, for instance, the great modification of *sooth* (contamination by touch), in Northern India, which apparently dates from the time the influence of the Mahomedans came to be felt.

The changes are even now daily growing, owing to the influences around, and not uniformly in different parts of the country. The Hindus undoubtedly are a conservative race, but not to the extent that is ordinarily supposed. In the ancient village communities of India an unwritten body of customary laws are observed, the origin of which is traced to the remotest times, and it is hence argued that the village communities have been always governed by usages and customs which have never changed. It is true that some usages and customs, favouring the growth of social organization of the kind prevalent in ancient times, and possibly having their earliest origin in this country, are yet found undying in certain parts of India, but with the growth of towns, with the disintegration of patriarchal families, with the growth of our modern land laws, revenue laws, sale laws, the so-called undying customs are fast dying out; and changes have gone on, and will still continue to go on, in accordance with the genius of the race, the surroundings of their position, and the climatic conditions under which they live.

Now, from this digression, to the subject in hand. As regards the first requirement of caste; *viz.*, (1). *A Hindu belonging to any one caste must not partake of certain kinds of food cooked by any one else but a member of his caste, or sometimes by one of the superior caste;* the rule of prohibited food must be taken to be still narrower. Brahmins, for instance, of Behar, cannot partake of food (rice and *dâl*) cooked by a Brahmin of Bengal, though of the same caste, nor can a Brahmin of Madras or Bombay do the same honor to his brethren of Bengal or Behar. The Bengal Brahmin, more saturated now with the progressive tendencies of the age, can, without offending caste prejudices, partake of food cooked by any Brahmin in India ; but with this exception, a Brahmin of one part of the country would not partake of food cooked by a Brahmin of a different part of the country. The same may be broadly stated to be the case with all other castes passing by the same name in different parts of the country, and when there are sub-sections of the same caste, the present prohibition against partaking of cooked food applies as well to those different sub-sections as to different castes. Thus, it is not the rule for the twelve different sections of Kayesthas in Northern India to partake of each other's food ; and, though perhaps the different sub-sections of Brahmins, Vaidyas and Kayesthas in Bengal treat each other more liberally in this respect, the Vedic Brahmins and Utter Rarhi (উত্তর রাঢ়ি) Kayesthas there still stand aloof from the other Brahmins and Kayesthas.

The rule, restricted in the way above indicated, is not, however, the same all over India as regards the kind of food, or the kind of touch (*sooth*) it shall bear. Throughout India, except in Madras, there are certain castes, water touched by whom can be used by the other castes (Brahmins included). They are *Jal-chal* (जल चल)—people whose water can be used; and below them are castes which are *Achal* (अचल)—people whose water cannot be used. *Jal-chal* and *Achal* are Bengali words of Sanskrit origin, and we have taken the liberty of using the words, as the corresponding idea in other parts of India is not expressed by a word, but by a periphrasis. Whether the Bengalis, old and young, should take it as a compliment or otherwise, we do not know, but they are all (their Brahmins inclusive) unless in very rare instances, now generally regarded as *Achal* by the rest of India. The line is drawn with such classes as *Gwalas* throughout India, *Nava-sak* in Bengal, below whom come the vast mass of Hindus who, though Hinduised, that is to say, though they form strata of the hierarchy of castes, are relegated to a position outside the sacred pale.* Are they content with this position? There is no open rebellion; and others,

* In the frontier districts of Punjab and Cashmere the distinction did not exist before the last twenty-five years, and even a Brahmin could use water fetched by a Mahomedan *Bhisti* (water-carrier) in his *mussuck* (leather vessel) for all purposes. A closer contact with Mahomedans and the growth of Sikhism, and possibly the conservation of the usage as it prevailed amongst the ancient Aryans,—between whom and the Afghans of the time on the other side there could hardly be any difference,—account for this. A closer relationship with the Hindus of other parts of India has now, within the memory of man, affected the usage.

mostly hill tribes, have been known, almost within historic times, to come in and take their position in the lowest stratum, but, as we shall show, there is a general attempt at upheaval which is very hopeful. Broadly stated, the sacred pale, as we have indicated it, ceases, with half-a-dozen castes below the Kayesthas in every part of India. Not only can water touched by these people be used, but their services, as domestic servants of a better sort, are acceptable as well; the Brahmin priests officiate at their ceremonials, and the Brahmins accept their gifts. In Madras, however, Brahmins can be served only by Brahmins, even to the extent of fetching water, and cleansing their houses. Except in Bengal, and in the Madras Presidency, it is allowable for all Hindus, Brahmins not excepted, to partake of all kinds of food—*puris* (पूरी) *tarkaris* (तरकारी), meat preparations of sorts, as also sweets, prepared by any one of these castes, with the exception of cooked rice (*bhât*) and (*dâl*). In Bengal, however, all classes, except one or two, who seem to have rebelled against Brahminical sway, and whose case we shall specially notice hereafter, take all kinds of food prepared by Brahmins. In Northern India, amongst certain superior classes, the rule would not allow *bhât* and *dâl* prepared by Brahmins, or by any one else not belonging to the caste, to be taken. In all parts of India, except Bengal, Hindus and Musulmans smoke, with different *hukas* of course, in the same *farcsh* (फराश), eat fruits together, and even sweets. The Punjabis and Cashmiri Brahmins are more tolerant of touch than other Hindus. The Mahomedan servants can carry from one place to another all kinds of their food (*bhât* and *dâl* included) if the vessels containing this food is wrapped up in a piece of *kambal* (woollen rug), or fastened to one end of a stick, the other end of which the bearer uses in carrying the load. It is doubtless a relic of an ancient Aryan custom, affected by the fiction of a barrier of *kambal* and wood (काष्ठ) introduced by the Sanhitas. One section of Kayesthas in Upper India (Saksena Kayesthas) employ Mahomedan servants in their households as *hukabardars*, and their tastes in the matter of food, and conspicuously in the use of household utensils, are distinctly Mahomedan.

In Bengal, as we have already seen, notwithstanding the rigidity of the earlier rules, almost all castes now tolerate * the partaking of food prepared by one of inferior caste, and even by Mlechchas and Musulmans, and even at the same table with them. In a few years more, when the influence of the educated classes shall have filtered down, as it promises very soon to do, it is probable, the so-called reaction notwithstanding, it will grow to be the rule, and not the infraction.

We said that below the classes whose "touched"

* (*i. e.*) Wink at the action of those who do, and do not, put them out of caste.

water can be used, come in the castes *Achal* (अचल), comprising the vast mass of Hindus, not less than two-thirds of the entire Hindu race, who, though Hinduised, that is to say, though they form the lowest strata of the hierarchy of caste, are relegated to a position outside the sacred pale. Whether these were not the original inhabitants of the country, who, after resisting the Brahminical influence as long as they could, were subsequently incorporated with the Hindu system, is an enquiry not pertinent to our present purpose. The question with which we are concerned is, whether they are content with their present position. They have always given the greatest number of converts to new religious systems introduced into India, and unquestionably, in times gone by, they have rebelled against Brahminical supremacy. We have a few instances showing such discontent in the social history of Bengal within the last few years. Only a few years ago, a Chief of an Independent Native State expressed such discontent with the position which his family and tribe, admitted by all to be Hindus, held among the Hindus of Bengal, and spent lakhs of rupees to bribe Pundits, and to maintain a party which he had succeeded in securing, and which promised to assist in getting him within the sacred pale. The attempt, through rousing some of the worst passions of men, in a *Dala-dali* in East Bengal, ultimately failed.

Perhaps here there would have been a better

chance of success by a manly revolt, as we find from the following :—The Jogis (the lower classes of weavers) who, unlike other Hindu castes in Bengal, bury their dead, revolted in a body against Brahminical supremacy. They declare that they are Brahmins, that they are entitled to the sacred thread, and to all the consideration due to Brahmins, and they have, by a unanimous resolution of the body, resolved to throw out of caste any one who shall partake of food prepared by any other caste, Brahmins included, or use water touched by them. A similar war has been declared by the *chundals* of East Bengal against the tyranny of the superior castes. There are also many other general attempts at the upheaval of the masses, though not in such a bold form amongst the other castes. In Bengal the Kayesthas, who, though generally regarded as Sudras, are one of the three superior classes forming the 'Bhadra-log,' gentlemen of the community, and who, from their present proud position of intellectual superiority, general attainments and wealth, might perhaps have done without a fresh accession of power, attempted to get themselves ranked as Kshetrias, to wear the sacred thread, and to curtail the period of mourning from 30 days to 15. The attempt collapsed, perhaps as unnecessary. Similar attempts have been made in Behar and the North-Western Provinces by Kayesthas, Kürmis, Koiris and other castes, under the influence of the teachings of the late Pandit Dyanund

Saraswati, and such an attempt has been very successful amongst the *Audha* Kürmis of Behar. By an unanimous resolution of the third Kayesth Conference held at Bankipur, in November last (1890), carried with acclamation, the Chittragupti Kayesthas of India declared themselves to be Kshettrias and Dwijas (द्वीज).

Such movements, where you level up, and not down, as most of our modern reformers do, appealing, as they do, at once to the *esprit de corps* of a whole community, should meet with the encouragement of all educated men, and a desire to rise should be stirred up wherever such a feeling is wanting.

We find, therefore, that other parts of India, except Bengal and Madras, still follow the ancient rule under which food cooked by the Sudras was not prohibited to be taken by the three regenerate classes, but have drawn a line at the classes comprising the Sudras of the present date, below which they regard touch as contamination: that they do not observe the *sooth*, as the orthodox Bengalis do, with regard to Mussalmans, so far as partaking of fruit, sweets, lemonade and ice-creams, and the smoking of *hukahs*, are concerned; that there is almost a successful revolt in Bengal against the rigidity of *sooth*; that this revolt will bring the Hindus of Bengal of the present date to a point nearer the injunctions of the Shastras in this matter. Outside Bengal, where the *sooth* principle was never so strong, it is hoped, that from the partaking of fruit, sweets and ice-cream together, to the partaking of dinner together at one *farash* (फरास), or table, will be but a step, and that it will not take long to introduce the change, which as we have said, will bring them nearer to the ancient Shastras, and thus one distinctive feature of modern caste, which is surely a great bar to the growth of fellowship and of a united people, will be done away with.

(2) *Interdict of Marriage amongst members of different Castes.* A Hindu must not marry outside his own caste; this is the second requirement of caste—a requirement, the breach of which is never tolerated by the Hindus, who consider the conservation of their caste system, nay, even their Hinduism, to be dependent on the rigid observance of the rule. On the other hand, it was only the other day that a Vice-Chancellor observed, in the course of his annual Convocation speech, before the assembled Senators and graduates of one of our universities, that India could never rise as a nation unless and until this interdict to marriages was done away with.

We shall examine facts here as elsewhere. In countries and amongst nations in which, and with whom, the interdict does not prevail, the rule is that, ordinarily, one seeks his wife in his own neighbourhood; marriages between distinct nationalities, or in very distant places, are exceptions, and not the rule. Amongst certain classes of Musalmans of the

Shiah sect, the rule is, never to go out of the family. These people are distinctly endogamous, if not for the reason which originally made people endogamous, for a reason akin to it—their dislike to let the daughter's share of the heritage go out of the family. Amongst the Mahomedans of India generally, the rule is for marriages to take place amongst the same *Kuff* (कुफ). Now a *Kuff* comprises Mahomedans of the same class, Sheikh, Syed or Malik, or Patan, living in a given number of villages. Marriages out of *Kuff* are considered *mesalliances.* The largeness of the Hindu population has also to be taken into consideration. There are castes which contain populations that would be equal to the present population of England, and exceed the population of Ireland, Scotland, or Arabia, in the ratio of two to one. Amongst Hindus, caste rules do not, of course, interdict marriages amongst the same caste, or, in certain cases, between sections of the same caste, comprising ordinarily hundreds of families. It is true that there are certain families, such as, in Bengal, families of Kulins, who would not descend to those who are not Kulins; and in other parts of India, where Kulinism does not prevail, there are certain families amongst whom considerations—not exactly caste considerations—prevail, restricting marriages to certain families of the same rank. It is also true to some extent, that people of the same caste who live in different parts of the country do not ordinarily intermarry. The Brahmins of Bengal do not intermarry with Brahmins of other parts of the country, nor the Kayesthas and other castes of Bengal with their respective castes in other parts of India. Again, amongst Brahmins of Bengal, the Rarhi Brahmins do not intermarry with the Varendras, or the Vaidics, or the Deccanese (Dakhinatwas). The Ballal-Seni Vaidhyas, who live in East Bengal, do not intermarry with the Lakhsman-Seni Vaidhyas of Westen Bengal, and the Kayesthas of Bengal who are sub-divided into four classes, (Utter Rarhi, Dakhin Rarhi, Bangojo and Barendro), do not of course intermarry. In Upper India, amongst the twelve sub-sections of the Kayesthas, intermarriage is interdicted. A Srivasthav cannot marry an Ambast, nor a Mathur a Saksena, and so on. The Rajputs have rules of their own, based more on family considerations than considerations of caste. In Bengal, again, Kulinism, now fast dying out, except amongst the Brahmins, made marriages more restricted; and amongst Bengal Brahmins, for the purposes of marriage, the Kulin and Bangsoj are almost two distinct castes; only the Bangsoj enjoys the privilege, which he oftentimes buys at a considerable sacrifice of wealth and of comfort to all the members of his family, of marrying his daughter to a Kulin Brahmin, by which process, however, he does not rise himself in the social scale, but only brings down his

Kulin son-in-law to the rank of Bangsoj. Except amongst the Kulin Brahmins,—and even amongst them, necessity having given rise to some amount of relaxation of the rigid rules, polygamy is now growing out of date, and a better state of things is springing up,—no practical difficulty is felt amongst the castes in the matter of marriage. The rules of consanguinity (prohibited degrees), more extended among the Hindus than among any other race in the world, are observed almost amongst all the castes, with, of course, some local variations, which always, with few exceptions, tend to make the prohibitions more extended. Thus, certain castes in Behar (Babhuns amongst others) do not marry in the *gotra* of their maternal grandfather. This, of course, is a limit within a limit, exogamy within endogamy, and exogamy to an extent hardly justifiable in its nature; and, perhaps, if the Hindus were left to themselves in the matter, the exogamous limit would be narrowed, and there would be a change before long in the rule under which marriages amongst persons of the same *gotra* in the upper classes are at present prohibited. The *gotra* restrictions do not prevail amongst the lower classes, some of them not having a *gotra* of their own, that is to say, not having included themselves with any of the Rishi *gotras*. The interdict amongst the Hindus, therefore, does not mean consanguineous marriages; and from the populousness of the caste it does not practically narrow the field of selection (the power of selection being in the parents, and there being no love marriages) to any appreciable or mischievous extent. Where, however, any real difficulties have been felt, the Hindus have not been behind-hand in solving the problem for themselves in their own way. We do not speak of marriages amongst the Bangsoj Brahmins of East Bengal, who are allowed by their caste-men in this respect an amount of latitude which introduces into their body wives from almost all castes, who by a fiction, pass as Brahmin girls; but in this connection we speak of intermarriages amongst the Vaidyas, Kayesthas and Sahus (Vaisyas or Sunris) in the district of Sylhet, and amongst Vaidyas and Kayesthas of the neighbouring districts of Chittagong and Tipperah, noticed above. In this case we find that, while the paucity of the numbers of these particular sorts (especially the highest) in the districts in question has made them relax the rule of caste as regards marriages, the *sooth* (touch) contamination rule, stronger than ever it was in Ancient India, has intervened to prevent their introducing the ancient and orthodox custom of *Anulom* marriages. We have also seen how the Vaisya Jains intermarry with the Vaisya Vaisnavas, the ritual in such cases being entirely Hindu, and the Brahmin priests officiate in the ceremony, no matter whether the bridegroom is Vaisnava, or Jain. The change here, if not as great as that implied in the marriage of Hindus and Mahomedans without loss of caste, very nearly carries the Hindus to a departure of that nature. Mixed marriages are also very common among the Bairagi Vaisnavas in Bengal, who do not pertain to any particular caste, except that the Bairagis, whose numbers find fresh accessions from all the castes in Bengal, are now being regarded by the Hindus as forming a caste by themselves. Marriages here, again, are mostly love-marriages. In Upper India, the illegitimate offspring, called Krishna Pakshis, are still forming themselves into distinct castes, sometimes according to the similarity of their birth, though it is not uncommon to find the Krishna Pakshis of fathers of similar caste, but of mothers belonging to dissimilar castes, marrying amongst themselves. In the early days of the Mahomedan conquest and settlement in India, the Mahomedans, who could not have all travelled to India with their wives, must have, to a very large extent, taken Hindu women, mostly perhaps of inferior caste, to wife, and the race of Eurasians has sprung up within the last 100 years from the connection of Europeans with the women of the country. Here, too, the same rule has prevailed. There are no cases known in which *Hindus themselves* have taken a Mahomedan or European to wife and yet continued to be Hindus. At the present day the Brahmos of Bengal, who though originally Hindus and belonging to some one caste, do not profess to respect caste, have introduced intermarriages among themselves, and a special Act of the Legislature (Act III of 1872) sanctions such marriages, if registered under the Act. There are perhaps, from three to four hundred marriages registered under the Act, which, sanctioning as it does most of the reforms which, with few reservations, are considered desirable by all educated men in India, *viz.*, marriages at proper ages, monogamy, intermarriages, widow marriages—would have been much more popular if there were not an inherent defect in it (born of unmeaning opposition, to which the Legislature in a weak moment yielded) under which persons marrying under the Act have to declare that they are not Hindus, &c., &c. Whether the addition of a ninth, to the legitimate forms of marriage amongst the Hindus, most of which are now obsolete, in a permissive way, would be an interference with the Hindu law of marriage, is a question with which we are not now concerned. If a strong body of Hindus desire to have such a relief, we do not see why the Legislature should deny it to them; but, at any rate, when the Legislature thought itself competent to enact such laws as the Dalhousie Act of 1850 and the Widow Marriage Act of 1856, and did not think that they were an interference with Hindu Law, or breaches of pledge, we do not see why it should be thought that to enact such a permissive civil law of marriage, applicable to all classes alike, would be an interference. *Nolens volens*, Bengalis, who have visited England, have to marry under the Act, and to declare, without perhaps attaching much importance to the declaration, yet nevertheless against their wishes, that they are not Hindus. But in a recent case a coach-and-four was driven through the very existence of the Act, so far as this class is concerned, under the presidency of His Highness the Maharaja of Vizianagram and the *elite* of Calcutta society, assisted by the Pundits of Bhatpara. We refer to the marriage of the daughter of Babu Surendra Nath Banerjee with Dr. U. C. Mookerjea of Her Majesty's Medical Service. Let us hope that our other England-returned Bengalis may prove as cautious reformers as Surendra Nath Banerjee, and as anxious to keep in touch with the Hindus as he. But we want the Act, nevertheless, in the amended form noted above, as the ultimate goal to which Hindu reformers ought to reach. The facts stated above show that, wherever necessity has arisen, intermarriages have taken place, but that such marriages have been *pritilom* in form.

Perhaps necessity has also arisen for further commingling of caste in this matter of marriage, and a cautious reform, which would doubtless meet with popular approval, would be the bringing about of marriages between distinct sections of the same caste.*

* There has already come into existence a "*Rahri Bango Sanmilíni Sobha*," the professed object of which is to bring

Thus there are twelve sub-sections of Kayesthas in Northern India, and as many sections of Brahmins. In Bengal there are three sub-divisions of Brahmins, four of Kayesthas, three of Vaidyas. This last caste, which, according to the census of 1872, counted 96,000 souls, counts only 92,000 according to the census of 1882, and for marriage purposes this population of 92,000 men divides itself into three sections, and the division causes much inconvenience. This inconvenience is being felt by all the people composing the caste, and if the educated leaders were only to try, an amalgamation might be easily brought about. Bringing about marriages between members of the same caste in different provinces ought not to be at all difficult. This, surely, would not be intermarriage, but a cautious progress towards that end, and on lines on which intermarriage may be a desirable change, acceptable to the people of India.

The *Anulom* is the form in accordance with the Shastras; the *Pritilom* has been the form in practice wherever intermarriages now exist, except amongst Rahri Bangsoj Brahmins of Bengal. The reformer will find that the *Anulom* is the form that will be more readily acceptable, and even if intermarriages do take place on any extensive scale, the *amour propre*

---

about an amalgamation amongst the *Rahris* and *Bangos* of Bengal.

of the caste will assert itself by adopting the *Anulom* and discarding the *Pritilom* form of marriage.

(3.) *The Supremacy of Brahmins in the Hierarchy of Caste.* A Hindu must admit that he belongs to stratum so and so, whilst in the highest stratum are the Brahmins. This is true, with but a slight exception. The exception, however, proves the rule. The Jains and Sikhs, though incorporated with the Hindu system, do not admit the supremacy of the Brahmins. Nevertheless, it is the case that these people have a distinct place assigned to them in the hierarchy of caste by the Brahmins and the adherents of the Brahminical system, and, by accepting the place assigned as a condition of incorporation with the Hindu system, they tacitly admit the superior position which the Brahmins occupy in the hierarchy. That these Brahmins, except in certain parts of the country, were always, and still are, the most intelligent people amongst the Hindus does not admit of a doubt. In Bengal they have taken the fullest advantage of the opportunities for progress presented to them, while their progress in the Bombay and Madras Presidencies ranks them among the foremost of the people in those parts of the country; and though their progress in other parts of India, especially Behar, has not been so rapid, yet relatively to other castes, they have not been intellectually backward. It is however, in advanced Bengal that Brahminical supremacy has always been the strongest. The worship of innumerable clay images of gods and goddesses in Bengal, unlike that in any other parts of the country, may have tended to keep up the supremacy, or that supremacy may have given rise to these innumerable *Pujahs*. It is also possible that these causes acted and reacted on each other. In Bengal, again, as in the rest of India, Sanscrit learning has been almost the monopoly of the Brahmins, and some of them have been exceptionally learned in *Smritis* (Hindu laws) and *Naya* (Logic). Whatever little sign of scholarship we find in Bengal, in the vernacular language of the Province in the Mahomedan period, we find confined almost exclusively to the Brahmins. From Vidyapati to Bharat Chandra and Kirtibas, all the Bengali poets, except one or two, were Brahmins, and it is one of them who has been the greatest of religious reformers in India. The Brahmins of Bengal have never touched the *amour propre* of other literate classes, who are here known as *Bhadralog* (gentlemen), and the influence of the Brahmins, exercised in conjunction with these classes, has maintained the hierarchy in a more developed form in Bengal than elsewhere in India. The institution of the Family Guru and Purohit in a more rigid form than elsewhere, also serves to preserve the Brahminical influence in Bengal. In Behar, where the Buddhistic system long prevailed, the Brahminical influence is the least felt, excepting in the Mithila country, where, perhaps, Buddhism was never very strong. Except in Bengal, Bombay and Madras, and excluding certain classes of Brahmins in Upper India, who have been progressing and keeping pace with the altered spirit of the times, such as the Kashmiri Pundits, elsewhere in India the Brahmins are regarded as poor beggars, to whom it is a merit, on occasions of *Shradh* and religious ceremonies, to give food and alms. They do not form a body politic with the other castes, as in Bengal, nor an exclusive class who disdain other classes, as in Madras.

We shall analyse into its component parts the idea of Brahminical supremacy in Bengal, as it is the strongest of its kind in India; but it is to be distinctly understood that the exercise of the various acts comprised in this complex idea in touch with the Brahmins as a body, is confined simply to a few of the upper classes, whose number cannot exceed more than a fourth of the population of India; for as to the rest, they are beneath the touch of the Brahmins, and scarcely any connection exists between them and the Brahmins as a class, except perhaps, that under the recognised Hindu system of the hierarchy of caste, one occupies the position at the apex, the other occupies the position at the base. These component parts are :—

1st.—Having to send for the family priests, or any of the class in cases of all *Puja-pat* (पजापाठ), and all ceremonies in a

Hindu's life; beginning with *Jatakarma* (birth ceremony), and ending with the *Shradh*, as also at times of all *Parvas* and annual *Shradhs*.

2nd.—Having to send for the family Guru for the purpose of initiation, and having to send for him from time to time to keep up the spiritual growth.

3rd.—Having to feed a number of Brahmins, beside the family priest and Guru, at all *Pujapat* and ceremonies.

4th.—The encouragement of Sanscrit learnning for those who can afford to do so, by bringing an assemblage of Pandits and making presents to each according to his rank.

5th.—Acknowledgment of Brahminical supremacy by all other castes, by having to bow down to Brahmins and receiving their *Asirbad* (आशीर्व्वाद) (benediction), in return.

The duty of sending for the family priest in all ceremonies, as required by head No. 1 of the above analysis; the duty of sending for the family Guru for the purpose of initiation, as required by head No. 2; the duty of acknowledging the supremacy of the Brahmins by bowing down to them, as in heading No. 5, are also required of the *Achals;* but the Brahmins who officiate as their priests (1) lose touch with their fellow Brahmins. The Vaisńava Gossamis alone act as their Gurus, (2) proving perhaps that there was no recognised Hindu method of initiation for them in Bengal before the days of Chaitanya. Bowing down (head No. 5) requires no touch whatever, but the Pariahs in the Presidency of Madras are denied even this. There is also a distinction observed among the *jal-chal* (जलचल) class, who are not *Bhadralog*, as regards the privilege of feeding Brahmins. As a privilege, it is very restricted.

The five heads of duties in the above analysis are also required of the Brahmins, only in their case the Guru and Purohit are of their own caste, and the Brahmins whom they have to feed are all their own kinsmen. These five requirements used to keep up the Brahmin's power in social matters and still serve to maintain it. The Guru and Purohit must act with their brother Brahmins; they must marry amongst other Brahmins, and must always keep touch with them; and they would *nolens volens*, have, to cease to act as Guru and Purohit, if their caste people insisted on their so doing, because of the social offending of any one of those in whose houses they minister, and a Hindu cannot keep touch with his caste-people if such ministrations cease. The influence of the whole body of Brahmins over the *jal-chal* castes, especially the class known as *Bhadralog* in Bengal, is thus kept up through the Guru and Purohit. Sometimes, too, the general body of Brahmins possess a good deal of influence either owing to their having wealth, or on the ground of the ignorance and prejudices of people around; so that, virtually, excepting in cases where the social influence of some other caste predominates in a particular locality—and this, too, is only possible by the influence in other respects which the caste can exercise over the Brahmins—the Brahmins are masters of the situation almost throughout Bengal. They can make a Hindu a non-Hindu, and a non-Hindu a Hindu, if all or even a large majority of them choose to do so. If the Brahmins were to set their faces against a certain movement, there would not be much chance of its permeating the masses, and if they were to set their faces against an individual, he must succumb if he chose to continue a Hindu. The family idol (*Salgram*) would remain unworshipped if peace were not to be made with the Brahmins, and so long as the *Salgram* was not worshipped, the aged mother would deny herself even a drop of water.

Now let us see how these matters are being affected by the progressive tendencies of the age. This progressive tendency is felt in three ways:—(1) By the spread of the influence of the educated Brahmins; (2) by the spread of education amongst the other castes; and (3) owing to the equality observed by the British Government in this country, by conferring on non-Brahmins positions which demand the respect of Brahmins.

It is quite unnecessary to enter into details regarding these. It is to be hoped that the influence of the educated and intelligent Brahmins may always be exercised to the social well-being of India and her people. It is a living Brahmin (may his life be long!)* who moved for widow marriage, and who still suffers excommunication from a section of his caste-people for the cause he advocates. As an indication of the tendency, we may mention that it is no longer the custom with these educated Brahmins to exact the Brahminical bow, and in return to make the *Asirbad*, but they merrily shake hands with people of other castes as equals. The outlandish mode of salutation has its use in this instance; for a native mode, indicative of equality, might, perhaps, not have been introduced and resorted to, without rousing suspicions and giving offence to the orthodox. The educated Brahmins, like other educated Indians, have given up all other prejudices, and very often meet people of other castes on equal terms at dinner tables. Thus the whole country is to be congratulated on the fact that a strong body amongst the Brahmins themselves are doing their best to promote equality.

But the spread of education amongst the other

* This was written before Pandit Vidyasagar's death.

castes is also a very important factor. The *pujapat* (पूजापाठ) has been minimised, the ceremonials have been greatly curtailed, and marriages and *shradhs*, which alone remain, and which must remain, are now less expensive, so far as expense on Brahmins is concerned, than they were. Even a Ganga Prasaud Sen Kabiraj now spends more money on hotel bills in his *pujahs*, for the entertainment of European guests, than on charges for the Brahminical feed. The Purohit finds his occupation gone and submits to the inevitable. His sons are, in some cases, the flower of our University—Rai Chand and Prem Chand Scholars and Professors in our colleges. The case is the same with the Guru. Several educated men have not been made *Guru mukh*, or initiated by the Guru. It will not be long before the caste will have to be analysed and interpreted without what we have now numbered, as its third requirement.

(4.) A *Hindu must abide by the rules of his caste*:— As to the marriageable age of girls, as to widow marriages, and as to going to sea and the use of the prohibited food.

(*a.*) As to the marriageable age of girls. The average marriageable age in India will be found to range between 10 and 12. Marriages at an earlier or a later age will be found to be more of the nature of exceptions than the rule. Mr. Malabari is not perhaps aware how, in Bengal, the marriageable age of girls is tending to rise. It is not the result of a sentimental reform, but the crude effect of certain crude causes. Fathers find it extremely difficult to find an eligible match for their girls, and when they have found one, to eke out the money that is required to secure the son-in-law. An Entrance "*fail*" has here his value; the Entrance "*pass*" sells dearer still; and a *graduate* sells very high indeed in the marriage market. Every University *honor* has its corresponding value, and for many persons with limited means, it is growing a question of the deepest concern how to marry their daughters, regard being had to the cruel custom that has seized hold of society. Ordinarily the highest pay in Government Service for an Indian is that of a Sub-Judge; and to dispose of five daughters would cost a Sub-Judge his life earnings, even if he were not extravagant in his habits. The difficulties in the case of those who live from hand to mouth are simply inconceivable, and as they are in their nature general, the caste rules have considerably modified the rule which insisted on marriages coming on before the age of puberty. Thirty years ago a Hindu of the *Bhadralog* class in Bengal would have lost caste if he had kept his daughter unmarried up to the age of puberty—the caste rules were never so strict in other parts of India. The offence is no longer visited with the punishment of ex-communication, and the feeling in such a case is one of pity and sympathy rather than of indignation. Public feeling and public opinion have thus changed, and, out of the difficulties experienced in getting daughters married, the marriageable age of girls is rising to the point which the reformers aim at. But perhaps the limit thus determined, from 10 to 14, is the extreme limit to which it will ever reach as long as there are not some very radical changes in other respects. There are now extant a few factors which conduce to early marriages. Perhaps these have not received due consideration from those who demand radical reform. (1) Every Hindu girl, whatever her parents' position in life, whatever her own qualifications for the matrimonial market, must be married once in her life. Old maids are unknown in India, except among the Kulin Brahmins of East Bengal, and even among them the class is fast dying out. It is ingrained in the Hindu mind; and even educated fathers and mothers, when they understand that the alternatives are between early marriage under disadvantageous circumstances, and late marriage, or possibly no marriage, do not hesitate, in the best interests of their child, in choosing the former; (2) unless there should be a social revolution of a very radical type, bringing in a free admixture of the sexes, and such an admixture as to make love-marriages, after the European fashion, possible, parents in this country will have to give their daughters in marriage. Now, if they are to choose, they would naturally like to do so at an earlier age rather than at a later one, when, perhaps, their choice might not agree with that of their ward, and thus difficulties might arise, which to a Hindu would be intolerable and perhaps insurmountable in their nature. Perhaps, under the circumstances, the best solution of the matter is that which it is receiving among the Bengal *Bhadralog* at the present date. It has at least this merit, that, while it does not overlook the above considerations, it is bringing on a slow and gradual reform, exactly in keeping with all the present surroundings of a Hindu's life. There is no tyranny of caste rules here.*

(*b.*) Widow marriages. It were well if some facts in connection with the subject of widow marriage in India were properly borne in mind. Is enforced widowhood general throughout India? If not, among what proportion of the Indian population is enforced widowhood the rule? The subject has been discussed as if enforced widowhood in India were not the exception but the rule. It is doubtless so in Bengal Proper, with its Hindu population of 23 millions; but outside Bengal the case is quite different. Take, for instance, Behar. It has a Hindu population of 18 millions. About 3

* The Hindu wife, after marriage, does not become the mistress of a household, but under the joint family system of the Hindus, even in its most restricted form, a member of her father-in-law's family, and she is naturally affiliated to her surroundings more readily at an earlier than at a later age.

millions, or a-sixth of these comprise the castes of Brahmins, Rajputs, Kshettris, Babhuns and Kayesthas, and widowhood is enforced amongst these castes only; widows in all castes below Kayesthas remarry in what is called the *shanghaí* form. Thus widow marriage prevails among five-sixths of the Hindu population, and, as widow marriage is permitted among the Mahomedan population, there is widow marriage among six-sevenths of the population of the Province, and enforced widowhood among a seventh only. This will be found to be the case in other parts of India. Thus, Bengal excepted, we have widow marriage among six-sevenths of the people, running back, in the case of Hindus, to times perhaps out of mind. It is the remnant of their ancient custom, called in Behar and Northern India *shanghaí* (from the Sanscrit word, *sanga*, companionship.) Widows of any age can remarry, though it is not perhaps considered good form for her to remarry when she has a number of grown up children, and is herself far advanced in life. The youngest brother of the deceased is the best husband the relict can choose; but her choice is never restricted. Her father, mother, and brothers can give her in marriage to any person of her caste, and she herself is allowed to choose.

The form is very simple. On the day appointed, the bridegroom goes with a few friends to the bride's house, and there, at night, in the presence of females of the caste, places vermillion on the forehead of the widow bride. There is a feast given to the Punchait, and next morning the bride goes to the bridegroom's house. The form, perhaps, is *Gandharva*. Except that vermillion has now taken the place of garlands, or it may be the relic of a form which prevailed in India before the eight Aryan forms. No Brahmins officiate, but nevertheless there is no distinction made in the rights of the issue to inherit, or in the position amongst the caste people of the offspring or their mother. They are in all these respects the same as those of the wife married in regular form, and of her offspring. The marriage entails no forfeiture, except that the guardianship of the children of the first marriage passes to the relations of the deceased husband, if they choose to accept the guardianship; but this would be the case whether the widow remarried, or chose to remain single, according to the strict interpretation of Hindu law. It is extremely doubtful whether our Legislature was in full possession of all the facts of this customary remarriage when it enacted Act XV of 1856; if it had been, perhaps the forfeiture clause in the Act would not have been enacted in the form in which it now is.

Pundit Vidyasagar's reform was called for in the interests of the Hindu people of Bengal, and of a seventh part of the population elsewhere in India. The rest did not require the reform: all that was needed was the conservation of their good old custom. There is, however, some fear that, surrounded as the castes are by the influence and example of castes which, in the hierarchy of caste, are admittedly their superior, the castes, or their Punchaits, might in an evil moment come to assume Brahminical pretensions, and discontinue a practice prevailing amongst them, which it will yet take those who have it not, hundreds of years fully to establish. It should be the care of educated Indians of all races and castes in India, to assist those of other castes to conserve this custom; perhaps it is of some moment, even for the purpose of the conservation of the custom adverted to above, that the widow marriage reform should spread amongst the upper classes; for it is the influence and example of the higher castes, comprised in this seventh part of the population of India, including as it does the majority of the educated in India, that tells directly or indirectly on the manners and customs of the Indian people as a whole, for otherwise, it is scarcely explicable how our Mahomedan neighbours of the better sort, almost throughout India, are coming to look on widow remarriages with disfavour.

But what about the spread of reform in the upper classes? It is a matter of regret that the prospect is not very cheering, and for this our reformers are, to some extent, to blame. I caution was needed in the matter of any reform, it was here. The reform, to be popularised and to permeate, should have been gradual, and if our reformers had confined themselves at the start, and for years to come, to the remarriage of virgin widows, the opposition would have gradually diminished. Orthodoxy would have had to yield, if not to reason and the Shastras, to that touch of nature which makes mankind wondrous kind; but the Shastras provide, and the Act provided, for remarriage of widows of all ages—virgin widows, widows with children, and widows on the shady side of life. Perhaps it would not have done for the Shastras and the Act to fix a limit; the limit should have been drawn in the practical carrying out of the reform; but it was as if good practical sense had deserted the reformers in the praiseworthy, but mistaken zeal with which they set themselves to act. In a part of the country where the reforming zeal had risen to the highest pitch, a widow belonging to a respectable family, who had a grown-up married daughter by a former husband, was remarried, and the reform movement gathered such powerful opposition around it, that, although it promised to be very popular here, it has since met with strong resistance to its further advance. There was a powerful revulsion of popular feeling, and that in quarters where nothing but sympathy was expected. It is curious to note that, in the part of the country referred to, the strongest opponents of the movement are the widows themselves. Perhaps the movement could still be made popular if a band of reformers were to work out the venerable Vidyasagar's reform in the way indicated; remarriages of virgin widows alone, or at most, of widows below twenty-five, without children.

(*c.*) Going to sea. Most of the castes are at the present moment engaged in solving this interesting question amongst themselves. Some of them have solved it in a way of their own. The Punjabis and the North-West Provinces men send their young men, and also their old, to England, accompanied by a Brahmin cook and provision for Hindu food, and thereafter give them the benefit of a presumption that they have always lived like Hindus and never touched any prohibited food. The enterprising Marwaries, conservative to a degree in all their habits and modes of life, have decided in a Punchait that there is no objection to crossing the *Kalapani*, and have established firms at Aden, and in China and Japan. The coolies every day migrate to Mauritius, to Madagascar, to Trinidad, and other places, and return to India and are admitted to caste. The parties of artisans who were taken to the London Exhibition did not lose caste on return to India. The Maharajahs visited England in numbers during the Jubilee, and, of course, nobody dared say anything against them. In the Madras and Bombay Presidencies, Hindus who have visited England have been admitted to caste after *Priaschit* (expiation.)

Thre has been a similar admission of an England-returned Bengali in the Vaidya caste; and the agitation in the caste, consequent thereon, has now well-nigh subsided; but, in general, the Bengali youths who went to England for their education are yet kept out of caste, and it is not likely that they will submit to *Priaschit* for admission to it. Say they:—"People "who cross the *Kalapani* to go to Burmah, to Ceylon, "and even to China and Japan, are not thrown out of "caste. Why should we be? It is allowable under "the Shastras to go to distant countries for the pur-"poses of education and commerce, and we have not "infringed the Shastras by crossing the *Kalapani*. "The only thing that can be said against us, is that "we have taken food at present prohibited by caste "rules while we were in England, but such things "are daily done by people who have never stirred out "of the country. 'How can you,' say they to their "opponents, 'grow into a prosperous and great nation "if you never stir out of your homes and when you "visit those who do so, with social ostracism?' "Perhaps the most rational of these opponents will "say; 'We admit that we are unreasonable to a "certain extent; but it is not your crossing the *Kala-*"*pani* we really object to. We object to your for-"getting the Hindu manners, habits, customs, and "the Hindu spirit, through a few years stay in "England. We object to your anti-Hindu garb and "anti-Hindu ways and anti-Hindu spirit. A Hindu "lives for others; you live for yourselves alone, un-"less you have a superfluity to bestow on others. "A Hindu abnegates self; you are nothing if not "self.'"

Perhaps this is a little too strong for the present day.

Thus, there were originally faults on both sides, but things are mending. A perfect good feeling is growing up on both sides. The England-returned Bengalis are now fully national in their spirit, and we hope the time is not far distant when the caste-people will see, that it will not do for them to ostracise some of the best of their men and the flower of their youth.

(*d.*) Use of prohibited food. We have shown that caste rules have grown very tolerant in this respect, and it is not unlikely that the only things which will be contraband to the future Indian table, will be beef and ham. That surely will be a compromise which will please all the gods!

IV.—THE HINDU FAMILY.

The subject will be treated under the following heads :—

I.—A sketch of the development of the Hindu family types—showing that it is not true that the evolution of the types through the intermediate stages has always taken place in the same way, or that the complex types always preceded the simple or individual types.

II.—The causes of the growth of the complex types out of the original simple, or individual type. Its effect in rendering Indian civilisation essentially altruistic.

III.—The three kinds of types as they actually exist. The word 'joint family,' used to denote the second and the third types, foreign to the Hindu laws.

IV.—A comparison of the three kinds of type, showing wherein each is wanting and how they supplement one another, with the conclusion that, unless the Hindus were to substitute a civilisation of a different type, for their own, the three must subsist side by side, one sometimes passing into another, the ultimate aim of all the three being the same.

V.—What changes have taken place, and what further changes are needed to perfect the types, and even to make the second and third types live.

I.

It is patent, even on a cursory observation, that certain changes are taking place, at the present day, in the family organisations of the Hindus. The nature of these changes, their causes and effects, and the question of what is required to preserve the structure, will be treated further on; in the meantime we shall begin by trying to show, so far as the imperfect glimpses of Hindu Society which we obtain from ancient records will help us to do so, that such changes have been in progress from the earliest times. This we do, not by way of apology for the present changes, but in order to establish a fact which negatives a position that has hitherto passed almost unchallenged, *viz.*, that the evolution of family types through the intermediate stages has always taken place in the same way, and that the complex types have always preceded the simpler, or individual, types. There is yet another object which we

extracted the soma-juice, and strained it through a woolen strainer and joined the husband in the performance of a sacrifice. We find in one of the hymns, "O ye gods! the married couple who prepare oblations together, who purify the soma-juice and mix it with milk.

"May they obtain food for their eating, and come united to the sacrifice. May they never have to go in quest of food.

"They do not make vain promises of offerings to the gods, nor withhold your praise. They worship you with their best offerings.

"Blest with youthful and adolescent offspring, they acquire gold, and they both attain to a mature age.

"The gods themselves court the worship of such a couple as are fond of sacrifices, and offer grateful food to the gods."

The picture here is of a couple not surrounded by other couples or groups of relations.

The simple rules of inheritance, which we gather from the following verses of the Rig-Veda, point to the same fact, and to the fact that the complex types had not up to that time come into existence.

"The father who has no son honours his son-in-law capable of begetting sons, and goes (*i. e.*, leaves his property) to the son of his daughter. The (sonless) father trusts in his daughter's offspring and lives content.

"A son does not give any of his father's property to a sister. He gives her away to be the wife of a husband. If a father and mother beget both son and daughter, then one (*i. e.*, the son) engages himself in the act and duties of his father, while the other (daughter) receives honour."

Thus, on the death of a man, whatever he left, went to the sons, the daughters being, until they were disposed of in marriage, maintained by the brothers. Failing sons, the property went to the daughter's son, Apparently what is now called a "joint family," had then no existence. There is, of course, no survivorship, nor any rule laid down for the heirship of the brother, or other kinsmen. The property is that of an individual, and not of a corporate body. It descends, under an invariable rule, to the daughter's son; and, so long as he is not born, it is in the hands, not of the daughter, but of the son-in-law, in trust for the daughter's son. There was, of course, not much to give, and these simple rules sufficed. It was not possible that, under the surrounding circumstances of their position, any other type should be in existence, or should then grow up among the Aryans. The struggle for existence had impelled them to come out of their native mountain homes, to a foreign country, where they had to fight for every inch of land with the aborigines. Each man lived for himself, and there was no room for benevolence, or the exercise of altruism. It was the religion of enmity, and not amity, that ruled men in their daily struggles with the non-Aryans, *Dasyas* (enemies); and not much co-operation, save that of soldiers, fighting side by side with soldiers, either compulsorily or otherwise, was anyhow absolutely necessary. The simple type does not easily change, and we find that it continued long amongst the Aryan Hindus. The sacrificial ceremonies of a *post*-Vedic period show what type prevailed centuries after the first arrival of the Aryans in India.

Every separate household is indicated by a separate altar; and it was the duty of every householder to have such an altar, with the sacrificial fire on it, as soon as he married, after his period of studentship was over. The ceremony was called the *Agni Adhana* or the bringing in of the sacred fire. One of the priests chosen for the occasion procured the fire, and set it on the *Garhapatya* fireplace. Towards sunset, the gods and manes having been invoked, the sacrificer and his wife entered the house, placed the two pieces of wood for the preservation of the fire, brought by the priest, on their laps, and performed certain propitiatory ceremonies. Such, again, is the ceremony of the gift of the cake. The householder is enjoined to observe these ceremonies in all cases.

There is no exception made in the case of a student marrying after his period of studentship was over, when his parents were yet living, a clear indication that he had to start a house of his own as soon as he married, notwithstanding that parents, elder brothers, and the like, were living. He thenceforward came to form a separate household, and had to perform all the duties of a householder.

With a settled state of things, however, and agriculture expanding, a change is indicated—brothers living with brothers, even after the death of the father; but such a state of things appears to have been looked upon with disfavour by the law-codifiers, whose ideal family was the type indicated in the Vedas. Thus Gautama, in one of his Sutras, says, "in partition, there is an increase of spiritual merit," referring, perhaps, to the performances of the duties of a householder in his own household with his wife. The change of type of which we here get an indistinct glimpse, necessitated some rules of partition; but they appear to have been as yet very crude, and not in the form in which they afterwards developed themselves. One of the modes of acquiring property *by usage* is said to have been the property of re-united co-parceners. The property of a re-united co-parcener going to the co-parcener, and the acquisition of property by a learned co-parcener by his own efforts, as not being liable to partition with his unlearned co-parceners, are indistinctly touched. The co-parceners thus referred to are brothers, as all the Sutras related to co-parcenary property are preceded by a Sutra regarding a brother's succession, wherein we find that the property of not reunited brothers, dying without issue, went to the eldest brother, a verse indicating the fact that the subject of a brother's succession was till then in a nebulous state.

In point of fact, the question of a brother's succession could arise only in very few cases, as there were sixteen kinds of sons, with or without any blood connection with the deceased, the claims of all of whom were recognised, and preceded that of the brother. The family in which the existence of these sixteen kinds of sons was possible, had not surely that kind of decorum in it in which different couples could live together, or in which the so-called 'joint family' of the day could exist as a flourishing type. The brother's right to succession could be again defeated by the widow, by raising a son, or even two sons, to the deceased.

All this points to the conclusion that a change was springing up which was not yet fully recognised or provided for, and was even yet looked on with disfavour.

A full and formal recognition of the growth of a more complex type of family, is not even to be found in the "Manu Sanhita"; but there is evidence to show that, side by side with the ancient simple type, a complex type was generally growing up; and the conservative portion of the community, Brahminical law-codifiers among the rest, were not at all inclined to favour this change. Like Gautama, the codifier in this instance in describing the comparative merit of brothers living together and brothers living separately by themselves, finds in favour of the ancient type, as will be seen from the following verse:—

"Thus they will either remain united, or they will with the view of getting spiritual merit, by the establishment of the five sacrifices in each household, become separated; for in a united state, one alone has to perform the five sacrifices for the household; others do not: so there is special merit in separation."

These five sacrifices, not the Vedic, emphatically called the five great sacrifices according to the Manu Sanhita, were (1) teaching and studying, called a sacrifice to the Supreme God (Brahman); (2) offerings of water to departed spirits; (3) burnt offerings to the minor gods; (4) offerings to ghosts; and (5) an ever-hospitable reception of guests, described as a "sacrifice to men."

Just as we have seen to have been the case at the preceding period, the student is enjoined to finish his studies—the period for the finishing of which appears to have been between 25 and 40 years of age—when he returned home, married and settled down as a householder. The sacrificial ceremonies of old have been replaced by other sacrifices and ceremonies. But the student is still enjoined to light the sacred fire, though this, too, appears no longer to be the universal practice. According to changed custom, if he be thirty, he generally takes for his wife a girl aged 12 years, and, if twenty-four, he can take for his wife even a girl aged only 8 years, though there are indications that girls remain unmarried even to a later age, and sometimes, when of age, marry bridegrooms younger than themselves, who have not yet reached the age of puberty. With the general rule of marriageable ages fixed in the Sanhita, it is clear that the girl-wife could not be fit to take charge of a separate household, and so a changed type of family must have arisen, though of this there is not yet a fuller recognition. It is only laid down in the chapter on Inheritance:—"On the return home of the brothers from foreign countries, after the death of the father, they shall divide his property amongst themselves, if they all wish it: else not."

"If the eldest brother be virtuous, and all like to remain united, the eldest alone shall take the whole property under his charge; the younger brothers shall respect him, as their father, and depend upon the elder brother for their food and raiment." And then follows the verse extolling the merit of partition.

The rule of succession remains unchanged. There is no conception of a corporate existence, or rule of survivorship. The widow takes under an invariable rule, before the father and brothers, as also the daughter; and the succession of all is postponed to the succession of various kinds of sons, still enumerated, though all excepting two are looked on with reprobation, and the widow still has the power of defeating the succession of the brothers effectually for all time, by raising a son to her deceased husband, though this, too, is condemned as not a meritorious custom.

The commentator, writing at a much later date construes this text, as laid down in the Sanhita regarding the raising of sons, as applicable only to those cases where the brother lived separate from his other brothers, as, according to the commentator, widows had no right to the property of the husband where he lived united with his brothers. But the commentary is comparatively modern, and furnishes an instance of how the texts of our laws were interpreted by the commentators in accordance with changed customs. There is no reference of the commentator's note in the Mitakshara, where all the other texts and commentaries are quoted, showing that Syana belonged to a later age than Vijaneshwar.

Even in the text of Yajnyavalka, on which the Mitakshara is expressly based, we find the postponement of the succession of the brothers to the widow and the daughter to be an invariable rule.

In the Vyasa Sanhita, the date of which is fixed by some at such a late date as the conquest of

India by the Muhammadans, without, however, any authority, as there are quotations from it in the text-books admittedly of an earlier date, and which must, at all events, be later in date than the rest of the Sanhitas, we find a fuller recognition of this growing complex family type as a social institution. In the second chapter of Vyasa Sanhita, the duties of a housewife are described. They are much the same as used to prevail, until, of late, in a Hindu household. She is enjoined, after finishing her morning duties, to do obeisance to her father-in-law, mother-in-law, and other elders of the family. In the Manu Sanhita, again, we find that the elder brother should look on the wife of his younger brother as a daughter, and the younger brother should look on the wife of an elder brother as a mother. Thus the complex type was being gradually recognised, and the duties of the several members composing it laid down in consonance with existing usages.

But the fullest recognition of the growing and the existent type, which had very generally taken the place of the older and simpler type, we find in the Mitakshara, in the rule as to the devolution of property which the author, following, of course, existent usages, lays down in his text. The author after describing the various texts regarding a widow's succession, lays down :—

" Therefore the right interpretation is this ; when a man who was separated from his co-heirs and not re-united with them, dies, leaving no male issue, his widow (if chaste) takes the estates in the first instance. For partition had been premised; and re-union will be subsequently considered."

Such a qualification to a rule of succession was necessary to suit the changed conditions of Hindu families, the prevalent type which had grown up, and which, bringing, as it did almost a change in domestic relationships, and possibly in the degrees of affection, had already effected a change in the usage as to the devolution of properties. The author of the Mitakshara recognises the change, and tries to reconcile it with the earlier texts. But the rule did not come to be the universal rule in India. The complex type grew up in Bengal, just as in the rest of India; but the growing practice either did not supersede the old invariable rule of succession, or, if it did, was soon abandoned, and the old rule restored.

We have thus laboured to show that, in India, the simpler type of a family—a man, his wife and children—was the earliest, and that the complex type, more than one couple and their children living together in a family, came into existence later on. We have hitherto referred to what (excepting the hymns of the Vedas) would be generally called 'Ancient Laws' of India.

The literature of the Hindus gives evidence only of a changed public opinion in favor of the growth of a more complex type. But neither in the "great epics," nor in the succeeding "dramas," does one find the picture of people in homely life living together in a so-called 'joint' family, a kind of negative evidence—and negative evidence is the only kind of evidence we can look for in this matter—that the type, or types, were not yet the prevalent ones. But they give as much prominence to other affections as to conjugal love, and hold them up to public admiration as much as love between man and wife. Sacrifice of self is what each preaches, and this is the solid basis on which the introduction and permanence of a complex type of family was possible. One of the earlier dramas, "Malati Madhava," tries to portray all kinds of affections in a single drama: and it is rather significant that, nevertheless, the 'complex group' is not there to be found. It is not that the types were not in existence at such a later date; but the educational effect of Hindu Literature was nevertheless necessary to foster their growth and to make them fashionable. The "great epics" teach, by introducing examples drawn from high life; yet it is doubtful whether any of the pictures in them are pictures of a complex family. It is true that, in the "Ramayana," we find the sons of Dasaratha living with him after their marriage and forming the same household with their father and mother; but this was the case of a royal family, and the epic is supposed by some to have been produced at a very much later date. In the "Mahabharata," the hundred sons of Dhritarastra live with him, and Durjodhan, as the eldest born of the blind king, is the chief among them; but there is nothing to indicate that the hundred brothers lived together, further than that they were all princes of the royal family getting maintenance out of the royal treasury. The Pandavs are a type the like of which is not found to have ever existed in India. The Jadavs are mentioned as living together, uncles, nephews, etc. The description, however, implies a clan rather than a family. Here, too, the case is that of a royal race.

In what we have said above, we are aware that we reverse the order in which Sir Henry Maine thought the family types to have originated. His idea is that the original family type was patriarchal and joint; and that the simplest type—that of the man, wife and children—had branched out of it. He refers specially to the Indian village community and Indian joint families as the vestiges of the earliest family type, and we have shown, by reference to the authorities which he recommends as helping in the enquiry, what the rudiments of the social state were before the joint family system came into existence in India.

II.

The questions now are (1): What were the causes, or rather changed conditions, that brought about, and helped the growth of this new complex social type? (2): How did it affect Indian society as a whole, from an industrial and economic point of view, and from a moral and political point of view? (3): What brought about the differentiation of the Bengal type from the same type in the rest of India?

(1) It is clear that the first glimpse we get of the growth of the new type, is at a time when India was changing from a state of militancy to a state of industrialism. The Aryans, who had fully settled in the country, had brought the non-Aryans under their sway. The non-Aryans were no longer the Dasyas, the blacks, the enemies, against whom the thunders of heaven were to be invoked, but a lower class of beings in the social order. The days of compulsory co-operation were gone by, and the days of voluntary co-operation for the peaceful pursuits of life,—foremost amongst them agriculture,—had arrived. (2) This was the beginning; but the fullest development of this type, the growth of which the "Manu Sanhita" vainly tries to resist, is synchronous with a formidable social and religious revolution in India. A new order of things had arisen. The religion in which self was partially predominant, had given place to a religion in which there was a total abnegation of self; it introduced new ideas of humanity, and rules and discipline which swept away many of the ancient landmarks. It also introduced monastic order, the first in India, which,

when practised by worldly men, would be socialism in essence. (3) And when this new order was gone, or grown obsolete, it left behind it ideas, the counterpart of which the reactionary conservatism came to claim as its own. Conservatism no longer disfavored the growth of a changed society and a changed type of family. The older family altar, where the sacrificial fire was to be lighted by the family at its start, had long ceased to exist, and, in its place, had grown other modes of worship. The Vedic sacrifices had given place to *Pujahs* of gods and goddesses in temples not specially intended for a household, or householder; but where a number of people, men and women, forming different and distinct couples, whether living in one family or in different families, might join in worship. Not only temples, but places of pilgrimage, had sprung up in imitation of the new cult, and the idea of incarnation, unknown to the old set of beliefs, had at once riveted the attention of the people. Legends were multiplied, and monastic orders were growing up; and the *summum bonum* of existence came to mean, not the *ego*, but the abnegation of the *ego*. The fullest recognition of the type by our Law Codes dates from this period, in spite of a protesting voice here and there.

So far as its effects on the growth of Indian civilisation were concerned, they can be summed up in a very few words. It rendered Indian civilisation essentially spiritualistic; its materialistic side being no longer in evidence amidst its growing spiritualistic character. Egotism yielded to altruism. The fault was that there was no harmony between the two.

The difference of the Bengal type from that of the rest of India, is in the legal incidents. In Bengal notwithstanding the existence of joint properties between brothers, the property of a deceased brother, dying without sons, goes to the widow and daughter, and daughter's son, and during his lifetime a united brother enjoys the absolute power of disposing of his property in any way he likes, to which, by construction, is added now the power of making a disposition of his property by will. Thus, whereas, in the rest of India, the property of brothers before separation, or after re-union, is a co-parcenary, in Bengal it is not so.

The reason of this difference is not far to seek. The complex type of family grew up here for reasons exactly similar; but in the pursuits which the men followed, there was more need of individual exertion than of co-operation of members of the family. There was less of agriculture, as an exclusive means of livelihood, amongst the upper, *i. e.*, literary classes than in the rest of India. Whether it is cause or effect, the agnatic tie here is less strong. Again, Bengal Proper, though so close to the cradle of Buddhism, does not appear to have ever had the revolution in its midst.

III.

Having shown that the types in India have changed, with surrounding circumstances, from the simple into the complex, as ancient records attest, we now come to the family types as they existed within the memory of man, and which are even now generally existent, notwithstanding the changes that have been going on.

We find three types co-existent. The simplest is that wherein the man, his wife, and young and unmarried children live together, the married sons going into separate establishments with their wives. The second is that in which the man, his wife, and all the children, young and unmarried, and married sons, with their wives and children, live together. The third comprises a number of men and their wives, with the children of all the couples, *plus* such widows and their children as may have been thrown on their hands by the death of the bread-winners—to whom might be added the aged and the crippled. The first, as an existent type, is the least numerous. It is being brought about by a close imitation of the European types, in some cases in which a similar imitation of European models in other things has taken place. The type was not wanting before in India; only wherever it existed, it was either the work of a step-mother of the type of 'Rani Kakayee' of the "Ramayana," or of disagreement between mother-in-law and daughter-in-law, of a type differing from the generality of these types in India. Such types of families are reprobated and condemned by the public opinion of Hindu society at large; the man is condemned as weak, hen-pecked, chicken-hearted, and the son as undutiful. This type has been so effectually supplanted by the other two types, that a few years ago scarcely a family would have been found to come under it, unless it had originated in a case of the kind adverted to above; and it may be said that the trial of this type, though the most ancient in India, in a true Hindu spirit, without risk or loss of those domestic affections which characterise all Hindu relations, has not yet been made under the changed conditions. It is possible that such trials will come soon. In many parts of India, the sons in government service, in the practice of a profession, live apart, with their wives and children, in a different place from their father's establishment, and it is only occasional visits that they can pay to the family residence. Gradually their numbers are increasing, and the type, growing up under such happier auspices, may perhaps be freed from its present stigma, and be looked on with favour, provided the domestic affections do not cease to exist with separate and remote living, and mutual aid is rendered when such aid is needed.

The second type would be the usual type, even when a complex family type had grown up, where there were no brothers or aged parents of the father living; and, as such, it must always have existed, side by side with the more complex groups. But it is evident, from the actual state of Hindu Society at the present day, that their numbers have been greatly added to, by an increased splitting up of the complex groups of the last type, compared with what formerly used to be the case. We have seen that the "Gutama Sutra" and "Manu Sanhita" refer to partition amongst brothers, and their splitting into separate households as an act of merit. Public opinion in this matter suffered a change later on, and, even within the memory of men now living, division amongst brothers was looked on with disapprobation. But the feeling in Bengal regarding this matter has again undergone a change, and the neighbours have now no opinion to express about it. They think only that the parties interested understand their own affairs best.

In the third group, the men stand to each other in the relation of brothers, cousins, uncles or nephews, or fathers and sons. The widows are probably sisters, sisters-in-law or aunts. The number is sometimes greater and sometimes less; but there is a limit beyond which the agglomeration does not go; especially in Bengal, where the splitting up is almost identical with separation of mess, and separation of dwellings, even in cases of members who have not gone away in search of work. In no case, however, will it be found that the diluted degree of blood relationship amongst the members of the complex family group, extends beyond the fourth degree; and the legal presumption, that, whenever a question of joint or separate familyship arises, whoever raises it, and in whatever degree he may be related to the deceased, the family is to be presumed 'joint' until the contrary is proved, finds no countenance in existing or past types of the Hindu family. Separation comes about naturally, and is as much the rule amongst the Hindus as amongst the other sons of Adam. The fact that the members are related beyond the third degree, might very well be taken as rebutting, *primâ facie*, the presumption that the normal condition of every Hindu family is 'joint,' even if the legal presumption be allowed to exist.

The term 'joint,' with reference to a family, or an agglomeration of persons living together, as contradistinguished from 'separate,' is not of the Hindu law. The Hindu law-lawyers, who were full of verbal subtleties, and with whom every expression was fully weighed, would never have thought of using an expression like this. The use of the expressions 'joint' and 'separate' with reference to families, and the legal presumptions about it, are exceedingly modern, and were brought about by the British Courts in India. The Hindu lawyers would have said, if the expression had been used in their presence, we know of *Ek-anna bhukta* (एकान्नभुक्त) brothers, brothers living in one mess; we know of separated (विभक्त) brothers; but how can you predicate of a family, that it is either joint or separate, where families, to be '*families*,' must always be joint. An anchorite lives by himself and has no family: so men must be with families, or without families; when they live together, they live in families. Men and women living together must form a family. To say that any number of men and women living together is a joint family, and to say that the family comes to be no longer 'joint,' but 'separate,' when they cease to live together, is to suppose that a man and his wife living by themselves, after the others have ceased to live with them, are not joined in a family. The word 'family,' with the idea which it is meant to convey, is entirely European. Its vernacular counterpart, in its present sense, is of exceedingly modern growth; yet one does not exactly understand wherein the idea consists. Has so-and-so a family? You reply, "yes," if he has any children; you reply "no," if he be married and has a wife, but no children. Suppose all these children are married and live in separate establishments of their own, and the man and his wife live by themselves, what would be your answer? And suppose, again, if he, on the death of his first wife, leaving him a number of children, were to marry again, and have children by his second wife, would he not have a family by his first wife, and another by his second? It would, perhaps, be wrong to enquire of a woman whether she has, or has not, a family. The primary idea, if it were to be used in the sense in which it has been translated to India, would, we suppose, be a man in a married state, with his wife living with a number of children, young and unmarried. That is, however, not the sense in which the word 'family' can be made applicable to all Indian types. The only point of contact is that all those who form a family must live together, and in that sense families must always be 'joint,' and it is not correct to predicate of some of them that they are 'joint' and of others that they are 'separate,' simply because the original number twenty-four in a group living together comes to be divided into eight groups of three each. The three, as forming a family, are still 'joint.' The division of Hindu law is not of the number of men and women, but of rights. There is a joint right of a number of individuals, and there is a division of the sum total of this right into 'individual rights.' They provide for only two kinds of division (*vivhaga*): division in the lifetime of the father, and division after the death of the father, amongst brothers—indicative of the fact that, even when the complex types had fully developed and had to be provided for, the only case which it was necessary to provide for, was the division amongst brothers, the largest group not then extending any further.

IV.

In what will follow, we shall, therefore, not use the word 'joint family' to distinguish the third, or the more complex type that is now to be found gradually prevalent in India.

We have shown that this type is disintegrating and passing into the second type, if not into the first. What are the causes?

The primary cause is the contact of Western civilisation with the civilisation that has developed in India, and the changed economic and moral conditions which this contact has introduced and is daily introducing. The genius of the Hindu race, which we have elsewhere said, disdains imitation, will keep them from adopting the Western type as their only unit of social organisation; and as the type, as we have seen, once existed here, and has been found wanting, and replaced by different types—though all this took place in the remotest past—there possibly exist reasons in the constitution of the Hindus and Hindu Society, why this change should not occur. Possibly again, through this contact between the civilisations of the East and West, there will grow the perfected types of the future, and the genius of the Hindus will create them.

Family organisations are the units of society, and ultimately of the political state. But though, perhaps, social organisations, the creation of brute, *plus* intelligent force, or of any other principle, were originally intended to preserve the *units*, the units of whatever state of society we may conceive of, can subsist only in subordination to the social aggregate. They are, again, the nursery for those qualities which social aggregates need.

Now, of the three kinds of type which we have described above, the first is more fitted for the development of the conjugal affections, the second for that of the filial affections, and the third, for that of brotherly affection. We do not speak of parental love; it is so natural and so little needs development, that it can exist under all conditions. All these affections need harmonious development. It is true that the development of any one kind of these affections, develops love on the whole, and chastens man. Yet it is possible that, in the development of some one of these affections, the claim of the others might be overlooked. Nowhere, again, is it more true that extremes meet. The best training ground for the conjugal affections might produce,—for little causes, which possibly would not be allowed to grow in shape and form under the other types,—discord and disagreement between man and wife; and unbrotherly hatred, grows in types which are deemed most fitted to develop brotherly love. The first type, again, is individualistic, the second patriarchal, and the third communistic.

The types will have to be further examined under two heads: First, in relation to the question whether free scope for individualism is possible under any of these conditions, and whether it finds a greater check under the last two types than under the first; and secondly, with regard to the subject of individual responsibility.

Now, is it true that any one kind of these organisations is based on individualism, (*i. e.*), where the authority of individual, even within such limits as the law imposes, is not checked or controlled by any external authority, or any considerations from inside? In the first of these organisations, which is European, the individual, if he is fit for anything and wishes to be happy, must sacrifice his individualism, in the sense indicated above, to considerations of the limited circle of beings around him. This he will also have to do in the case of the other two kinds of organisation noted above. In the second, the individual father under whose authority all live, must, in order to be happy and to render others happy, sacrifice his individualism to considerations of the ideas, feelings, even the whims and caprices, of the individuals by whom he is surrounded.

In the third type, which is a nearer approximation to the European idea of a 'commune,' with this difference, that, whereas in a commune like that which Fourier thought of, the individuals need not be allied by blood, or by marriage—the kind of organisation, which, as a family group, is common in India, is based on such relationship—the '*karta*,' or the head (manager) of the family, whoever he may be, and it is ordinarily seen that the choice devolves on the individual of the group who has the best intelligence and tact, must sacrifice his complete individuality, even including the individual considerations of those of the group with whom he is more intimately connected, for considerations of the ideas, the feelings, and even the idiosyncracies of the larger circle around him.

The difference between the possible limits of individualism under the different types is merely one of degree, not of kind. This sacrifice of individualism, which, in its highest development, comes to be the moral virtue of self-sacrifice, is, therefore, the basis on which family organisations, however simple, must be necessarily based. But, whatever scope these different kinds of organisation present for the development of individualism, individualism everywhere receives a check from the social aggregate. This check is, of course, different in different forms of that aggregate. In India, it is in the first place imposed by the rules and usages of caste over the social units. In Europe conventionalism rules. A large class of people are always found there to be rising against the tyranny of social forms, just as many people here in India, rise every now and then against the usages and rules of caste. In both cases they may revolt against the present, but they will not—we may, in passing, say—shut out the future. It indicates a principle. It means that, as we proceed higher and higher, the units, in whatever form of family organisation they present themselves, must sacrifice their individualisms to considerations of the ideas, thoughts, and even idiosyncracies and prejudices of the social aggregate, in whatever form it exists. In archaic forms there is not a close distinction between what ought to be the restraints of law, and restraints outside the law, (*i. e.*), restraints of social forms. Gradually the two are separated in all developed forms, and both grow with the growth of these forms. So while, on one side, "individualism" finds a check imposed upon it by the social forms, it also receives a check, on the other from the growing laws. As matters look, the "coming slavery" will in time be complete.

But individualism checked and restrained is one thing, and the happiness of the individual checked and restrained is another. The object of all sound and reasonable checks must be the increase of human happiness in the aggregate, and so in parts; and any form calculated to diminish this happiness must necessarily be imperfect. If the second and third types are destined to exist, they will only exist in a progressive state of society, where they do not, in any way, restrain individual happiness. We shall show hereafter that this restraint is not at all necessary for their existence.

It must be conceded that, under existing conditions, a sense of individual responsibility does not grow to the same extent under the second and third types, as under the first. They are less favourable for such growth. Perhaps the deficiency is compensated by the fuller growth of responsibility in the head member, and in the growth in him of a certain amount of power to govern his fellow men. There is also a division of work and a nice apprenticeship for those who are to come next. There is also the growth of an honest ambition to take the place of the head member when the time for it comes.

But, with all that, the last two types, especially the third, give rise to a class, called by Englishmen and some English-educated natives, "drones," in derogation of a class of men who will not labour for what they would eat. Their number is fast decreasing under the present economic conditions, and, even where they still exist, they are receiving a kind of treatment on all hands, which is not calculated to foster the further growth of the class. The fact is, public opinion in this matter has, to a great extent, changed. A man would not, under our past standard, have been considered as doing his duty by a dependent of this class, unless he treated him and his, in all respects, as equal to himself and to his own. The same is not the case now.

But there are classes of relations whose claims a Hindu, as long as he remains a Hindu, cannot overlook. There are the aged, the cripple, the helpless widows and orphans of his own kith and kin, with whom, if he has a morsel for himself and his, it must always be his duty to divide. And it is not possible, in the nature of things, unless great violence were to be done to our national feelings, that the first type could long remain as a type of that class, if the duties which the Hindu regards as sacred, were to be attended to. Brothers and sisters of an unripe age might be left orphans by the death of fathers and mothers. Brothers might have left children as orphans, with no widows (mothers) to attend to them. A widowed sister might seek protection under the brother's roof; an aged father and mother might have to be looked after. Unless public opinion in this country were to suffer a tremendous change, a close imitation of foreign modes of rendering assistance in these cases would never commend itself to us. An individual dies, possibly without being able to provide for his immediate environments, with the consoling thought that others will take his place. A brother or a nephew on whose education and support he has spent all his little means, as the best investment for the future, comes to be a successful man of business. What would the public think, what would he himself feel, unless he were a social reprobate, if he were not to take under his wing those from whom he had received assistance in the days of his need. Here the individual type gives way and passes into the other types

So it is impossible to say what, under varying circumstances, the type or types would be. Of course, circumstances tending to weaken responsibility should not exist. Education, a healthy public opinion, appropriate assimilation of ideas drawn from Western civilisation, and consequent changes in the condition of the peculiarly Indian types, should be relied on to bring about this sense of individual responsibility.

In a poor country like India, cheapness is a recommendation in many matters, and in family organisations amongst the rest. In this respect, the third type, excels the other types: and this was one of the reasons why, perhaps, it commended itself to almost universal adoption. It was cheap as regards expenditure of money, as regards expenditure of physical labour, as regards expenditure of mental labour, and it enabled the people included under it to devote their time to the things which most interested them, freeing their minds, as it did, from the almost engrossing cares and anxieties of a household.

It is strange that the first splitting up of the complex family type in this country appears to have been due to the growing poverty of the people. This arose from the fact that the bread-winner in a family, under the abnormal conditions which the complex type had assumed, was, in many cases, a single individual, and it was not cheapness that recommended the split, but a desire on the part of such bread-winner to curtail expenses. It will primarily be a desire for cheapness, again, which, under better conditions and better education, will recommend the second and third types to our people, and perpetuate them as Indian types, with our abnormal growth of population, and with the consequent ever growing poverty of our people.

V.

But, like many other institutions in this country, the types are undergoing changes, and assuming forms, more suited to present circumstances. It is quite in the order of things that, for the moment, the principle of *egoism* should appear to have an undue preponderance, and altruism to have lost its hold. A reaction, as in so many other things, is coming on, but the rehabilitation of altruism in the old archaic forms, more in this than, perhaps, in other things, will be found impossible; and a harmonious blending of the two—the assimilation of whatever there is good and beautiful in the form of the West with the types of the East—may ultimately be depended on: The perfected types of our future civilisation will be the forms thus developed.

These perfected types, we hold, are such as are the best fields for the development of all the affections of man and woman, and for their intellectual growth. The types as we have said will differ according to their varying circumstances: they will remain side by side, one sometimes passing into another. But the goal must be the same; the conditions for the development of the individuals, must be the same within such restraints as law or society imposes, and these restraints, we suppose, are ultimately destined to be only such as are calculated to produce the greatest happiness of the greatest number. All other restraints on the growth or happiness of individuals, where they exist, must necessarily come to an end. What are the changes from which we can expect the evolution of the perfected types, with our present type as a basis? Primarily they will be found in what follows.

Nowhere is altruism shown to greater perfection in the complex types than in our women. They do not know what self is. It is the care of the household that engrosses their attention. Everything of the best is for others, and not for the mistress of the house. With servants and maids in number to do her bidding, the woman is a willing drudge from a very early hour of the morning to the latest hour of night; her husband's remonstrance she heeds not; she cannot change her habits; she sits up at night to tend the sick. The slander has been often repeated, that she is fond of ornaments. The best of the type aims at being the least costly to the family; and certainly she, as a wife, is less costly to her husband than wives under other types of civilisation. She is content with whatever the family can afford to give her, equally with the rest. The class has not yet died out. Others amongst the class prized the ornaments, not for their own sake, but as a means to an end. They were held good as a provision against a rainy day. It is the woman who practically manages all the affairs of the household, sweetens the life of all the members of the family, harmonises all interests by universal love, and preserves, by her example, in all respects, the moral tone of the house.

When a disruption comes in a family of complex type, the neighbours say the women are at the bottom of it, and this is for some time currently believed ; but the secret comes out ; it is the men who are the cause, and not the women, who have warded off the day of disruption as long as they could. The complex type could not exist for a day, if the women did not keep it up.

What, again, could be a better school for the training of the girl wife of India for being a dutiful wife, a dutiful mother, a dutiful mistress of the household, than the schooling she receives from the mother-in-law. Cases have of late occurred here and there in which the Hindu mother-in-law has been held up as a tyrant to their son's wife. A greater calumny could not be uttered. Every Hindu knows that one of the earliest enquiries made when a girl has to be married is whether there is a mother-in-law ; and every one hesitates to pass her in marriage into a family where there is no mother-in-law, unless he is satisfied that there is some one as good amongst the female inmates of the household to take care of her. The mother-in-law, as a general rule, loves the daughter-in-law as a daughter; and the daughter-in-law pays back such love with true filial affection. But the subject of the Hindu family is a sealed chapter to all but the nearest relations; and one or two stray cases that have come of late before the Police Magistracy, of an extremely un-Hindu and obnoxious kind, have, to a certain extent, influenced public opinion. Those amongst the Hindus who were silly enough to join in such cry, must consent to change many of their social institutions all at once, if they conscientiously believe that the mother-in-law is the tyrant she is represented to be.

It is said that our women are not fit companions for our men. Perhaps it tickles the vanity of our young men, who have always a high opinion of themselves, to say so. The case is the reverse. Our men are immeasurably below our women. It would, in many cases, do them good to sit at their feet, and learn from them lessons of virtue and unselfishness. Perhaps the ideal of our women is too high for them to reach. But surely, if they cared for their own happiness in the long run, or the happiness of those around them, nay, of the society in which they live, they would not think of supplanting the present type of woman by one whose idea of a family would be drawn from foreign models; who would not think of a family until their husbands had given them a separate establishment to rule; who would think that the only duty of their husbands was duty to their wives in the first place and their children in the next; who would assert rights in accordance with the rights of women in other countries, and who would be sticklers in etiquette, according to foreign models, based on their second-hand knowledge derived from etiquette books. They would not hanker after a type whose taste for dress and finery would exceed the means of their husbands; who would think it superfine to say that they never knew how to cook, or how to do this or that,—hundreds of domestic duties for which women alone are fitted; nay, what is worse, who would consider it beneath them to do everything for their children. Our girls, our women, must be educated to a higher standard; but that education must be on a national basis. We are by no means in favour of restricting that education in any way. Science, mathematics language and literature are as much for them as for the men; the education which can alone fit them to take in hand the education of the children must be of the highest kind. If some of them are ambitious of obtaining University degrees, there is nothing to be said against it; but what should be jealously guarded against in the higher education of our women, more than in that of our men, is the allowing their minds to be formed in a way in which foreign ideas (especially this of the family type) would alone be adopted. There are few novels, for instance, in the English language, or for the matter of that, in the Bengalee language either, in close imitation thereof, wherein the protraiture is not that of conjugal love alone; other domestic affections scarcely find a place therein. In English novels the pictures are drawn from life; and the family types that are the subjects, are of the sort that prevails in Europe. There is no excuse for their existence in Bengal. Too much of this is sure to make girls disdain our Indian types, and is calculated to render them unhappy under their present conditions.

But what our Indian women want—and this is a subject which should not be overlooked in the education of our girls,—are those graces and female accomplishments which render life—always full of care and anxieties, where misery and happiness are almost equally balanced from day to day, from hour to hour —a little happier. The poetry, the music, the æsthetics, the innocent amusements, the little diversions which take away from our loads of care and morose thoughts, we require under all types, simple or complex.

There were the *Pujahs*, with their little amusements and their excitements; there were frequent ceremonies connected with birth, with tonsure, with marriages and a hundred other occasions, with amusement for the young and excitement for the old; there were the *Britas* for the women, prescribed for almost every month. The *Dharemghaut*, in the end of Bysak, with an expensive finale in the fourth year, when, throughout the month, the lady who performed the *Brita*, had to provide the best and the choicest food for the whole household, in addition to Brahmins, *Gayatis* (agnates) and *Bundhu* (cognates), men living outside the family; the *Jamai-susti*, when, in the month of Jait, the sons-in-law of the family were to be presented with the best clothes and choicest food, with flower wreaths, and knick-knacks of sorts, engrossing the attention of the ladies of the house for a month previous; the *Bhrata-ditya*, occurring ordinarily in the month of Kartic, when the thought of all women was to do the like by their brothers. These and a hundred other little things of the kind were taken advantage of by the Hindus for diversion, amusement, excitement, as also for the exercise of affection and devotional feelings. There were *Jatras*, and *Puthi Pat*, to the infinite amusement of young and old. Alas! these things do not now amuse! but have we been able to substitute other and more rational amusements in their stead? Judging from what we see, there is something in the observation that, wherever English education has permeated to any extent in India, the people are growing sombre and gloomy. There is no 'go'; no life; no combination of work and play; and, what is worse, there is no rational amusement in the family. Our young men play cards; our young women play cards, each in their separate domains. There is a tennis court outside in some houses;

young men, as well as old, sometimes join; but there is no provision whatever for the young women taking any healthy exercise. The duties attended to by their predecessors were of a nature which required bodily labour, and served for exercise, and kept the females in health; these duties are in many cases no longer required of our females, and, unless healthy exercises of some kind are to be substituted, it must tell against their health. Gardening, for the raising of vegetables, or flowers and fruits, was an interesting occupation practised by Hindu ladies. Is there any reason why it should be given up where its practice is possible? Public opinion bans this; public opinion bans music; public opinion bans the mixing of old and young; public opinion bans the presence of the young housewives before their fathers-in-law, and even their talking with the old women of the family. Public opinion, however, is undergoing a healthy change; and though people change with great difficulty in some of these respects, there is hope of alteration for the better.

In many enlightened families, daughters-in-law are treated in all respects as daughters; they are no longer enjoined to keep themselves secluded from the presence of their fathers-in-law, or uncles-in-law, or the brothers and cousins of their husband, except their elder brothers or elder cousins. There is also a bar to the wife appearing before the husband in the presence of the elder male members of the family. If the complex types are to survive under present conditions, these bars, no doubt, will soon cease to exist. Gradually, too, in places where such bars existed before, they are dying out in regard to the ladies taking an occasional airing in carriages with their husbands, fathers, fathers-in-law and brothers. In villages, even in Bengal, women do not live the secluded life which foreigners think they do. They go out very freely in company with the elder female members of the family. Of course, there is no bar to a young female appearing before her father's relations; and the whole of the village people, though of different castes, are held to be thus related, and her father's intimate friends.

There is no bar to their going to distant places of pilgrimage in company with their male relations. Even railway travelling is doing a good deal to demolish the *Purda* amongst the Hindus of the upper middle, lower middle and poorer classes. There is scarcely any *Purda* below a certain rank; though, perhaps—and in this instance again, the example of the upper classes is found catching—the first pretension to gentility consists in making the females of one's family *Purdanishins*.

But the question of the *Purda* is likely very soon to adjust itself in the way we have indicated above. There are obstacles, and pretty formidable ones too—we need not enumerate them—to its extending further, at least for many years to come.

The family residences are indexes of the family types of social institutions, and of the kind of happiness prevalent therein. In the Presidency of Bombay and Madras, where no special *Purda* seclusion is provided, there is only one courtyard in a house. In Bengal there are generally two, sometimes three, and sometimes four. They are ordinarily those of the male and the female apartments. The plan of Indian houses, especially in towns, is changing. There are the courtyards, as of old; but ordinarily the lower storey is used by men as a place of business, and the upper storey by females, as also for sleeping rooms. There are drawing-rooms, both inside and outside, and, in some cases, dining rooms are coming into fashion; while separate suites of apartments are being provided for each married couple. Necessities and regard to convenience will suggest some other changes in the plan of residences as time goes on.

The drawing-room upstairs, where the females of the family ordinarily congregate, is now in most cases furnished with a piano, or a harmonium; and the music, in solo or in concert, practised by the Hindu ladies of the family, as also the sweet vocal music, are indeed becoming charming. The violin and *sitar* are also instruments to which they are giving attention. They practise drawing, and some of them are growing apt designers of beautiful things. Here, then, should father, mother, sons, daughters-in-law and daughters meet to enjoy their evening. Family billiards, very simple games, cards, draughts, &c., the children giving occasional little performances of their own, with the aid of their immediate elders, might advantageously follow, to enliven the evenings; and an occasional pic-nic outside the house might be given, by way of diversion. The æsthetics of the drawing-room and of the other rooms and their contents, are subjects in regard to which a happy emulation (a feeling which even now exists) should arise between family and family.

But there is a little thing, which, except in houses marked as *anglicised*, is still to come;—the taking of meals together. The Hindus are a people eminently fitted for domestic enjoyment; and a habit of this kind, which adds to the sweetness of the meal, will not be entirely a novel practice. A Hindu enjoys his meals best when he has a number of children to sit and partake of food out of the same dishes with him; the lady mother, or aunt, or, if they do not happen to exist, the lady wife, with the daughters, sitting by, and keeping up chatty conversation, while they ask you to take a little of this or that, and minister to the enjoyment of the meal in diverse ways. In days of yore, when the grandfathers and fathers of the present generation were young men, it used to be whispered against them, that they, on the sly, sometimes partook of the evening meal with their wives. The practice, then, should be a little extended, and when the barriers we have spoken of are gone, as they are destined to go, this one innovation should come in. No doubt, the females would feel some awkwardness, and it is pretty well known that, in societies where the practice exists, the ladies themselves go half-fed when they sit with the males, and it is the males who, so far as the actual eating is concerned, do their best. This may be a good reason for not introducing the association of males and females at meals: but, perhaps, this disadvantage would be found to be out-weighed by many advantages. For a business man, whose time is fully occupied, the only time which he can give to his family, without detriment to his work, is the time for meals, and perhaps an occasional evening; and while the enjoyment of meals will be added to, by the presence of all the members (male and female), it will keep these business men in the family *en courant* with the thoughts of those around them.

There are a few other things which must mend, if the complex type is to live. Our young and old appear to have nothing in common between them. The old people hardly ever exchange their thoughts with the young; and this is a great bar to their mutual happiness. The Hindu idea about it is correct enough. The father, when the son is of age, must treat him as a friend; but the Hindu practice is somewhat different. This reserve, in most cases, between the father and sons, has grown by habit into second nature

Lastly, it is said that the moral atmosphere of our homes is not good for the children. It is a calumny which often goes unchallenged, and every repetition adds to its supposed truth. A better field for the cultivation of the affections which ennoble human nature; a better field for teaching the young to be unselfish, when the children of the bread-winner are treated alike with the rest; a better field for teaching the young to 'do to others as they would be done by' cannot be conceived. A moral atmosphere of affection and unselfishness pervades the whole structure. What, perhaps, is now vanishing, without a proper substitute taking its place, is an air of devotion and religiousness of faith, from day to day.

We cannot say that, for the better development of the intellect of the children, changes are not required. We want mothers educated both in geography and in history, in the elementary truths of science, and in every-day common affairs of life, to take charge of the early days of our children; females, who can return correct answers to the many questions which the inquisitiveness of children prompts them to ask of their elders.

But the growing sense of individual responsibility must be fully developed if the complex type is to live, and to be perfected as one of the types of the future. Every adult male member must contribute equally to the common family expense, including not only the expense of the common mess, but all the expenses of the children, with that of their education. The practice that has been growing up of recent years in some of the families of complex types, of unequal treatment of the children according to the means of their parents, cannot be sufficiently condemned. It was unknown even at a time within the memory of man. They should be allowed to live together only under conditions in which the demoralising effects of such unequal treatment cannot exist. It is better that the family should break up, at whatever hardship to individual members, than that such a state of things should be allowed to exist. The contribution for the purposes noted above being made, each one should retain his savings for his own use. For the individual wants of himself and of his wife, he must look to himself as also to the making of as good a provision for himself, his wife, and his children as he can, consistently with his means. Changes in the complex group in Bengal are taking place in this direction.

The changes have not occurred to the same extent in all parts of India. In places where the causes have been more potent and have operated for a greater length of time, you find greater changes than in others, Bengal has been more affected than the rest of India; and parts of Bengal, nearer the capital, more than other parts. It would be to as little purpose to ask of my countrymen to resist the changes, as to ask them to resist a rising tide. All that we can do, is o see that the solid foundation is not swept away by our unwise resistance. Whenever changes spring up, it behoves every Indian, man and woman, to try to mould and adopt them as fast as they can consistently with the preservation of their existing institutions,—retaining as much of altruism as they can, and admitting individualism and egoism wherever necessary, and thus working out a harmonious whole, the like of which does not yet exist in this world.

V.—THE GROWTH OF AN INDIAN NATION.

"India is all past, and, I may almost say, has no future,"* says Professor Seeley, and the same remark, in the same or in similar words, had been made by a host of his predecessors, who, observing the high stage of civilization to which India had once reached, and the stagnation of the present day, thought the remark appropriate, and the prophecy justifiable.

It is interesting to observe the various phases through which the minds of educated Indians have passed even in the matter of this remark. The earliest stage was to take the result of the European thought, even though not strictly scientific, on trust. The high authority of the Professor and of his predecessors was sufficient to secure its unquestioning acceptance—and it led, however temporarily, to a demoralizing quietism, bred of that philosophy of *Kismut*, from which, consciously or unconsciously,

* *Vide* "Expansion of England," p. 176.

even the intelligent and educated amongst us cannot always free themselves. It led intelligent and educated men to despise the present and the future, and simply, not to live in the past, but to talk of India of the past, and her glories of the past, and see nothing in the progress of the world during the last thousand years or so. With minds which ranked above the philosophy of *Kismut*, and which could not ignore the phenomena of progress around them, it became the fashion to affect a sort of cosmopolitanism, which, however, is no better than cynicism, *minus* its essential virtues so far as one's own country is concerned, and the result was, none the less, demoralizing quietism. But it is hardly possible that, surrounded as they are with the signs of progress, the Indians should quietly accept the destiny foreshadowed for them in the remark quoted above. The reaction came, and Indians thought that, if that was their inevitable destiny—only a dead past, however glorious a chapter in the history of mankind, and no future—it were well if India were at the bottom of the Indian Ocean. Who will say that the impious thought involved in the re-actionary stage, has not a more manly tone about it, than the belief in *Kismut* and consequent inaction. Out of the discontent which it clearly indicated, educated and intelligent Indians have come to question the soundness of Professor Seeley's remarks, and, happily, to ask themselves, why the Indians of to-day, inheritors as they are of a unique civilization of the past, and in actual contact, as they are, with the materialistic civilization of the present, should not be able to make for themselves a grand future. If, they argue, it is now said of India, that it is all past, and has no future, was it not once said of Italy:—"L'Italie n'est qu'une expression Geographique," and believed, even by such a celebrated diplomatist as Metternich, that every spark of vitality had fled from her.

It is the fashion to speak of a Greek civilization, a Roman civilization; to speak of them as dead and gone, and to compare them with the living civilization of present Europe, as if the world's progress from the earliest times to the present, were not one continuous whole, but marked off with full-stops at the different periods indicated. Prejudices are often retained in words, in the mode of treatment of a subject, and thus imperceptibly, in thought, even after a contrary truth has been fully recognized; and though history amply illustrates and proves the fact that the present European civilization,—that is, the progress of mankind of the nineteenth century,—was evolved out of Greek, Roman, nay Indian civilizations of the earlier ages of mankind, it is the rule to speak of the one as dead, and the other as a living entity by itself, disjointed from, and unconnected with, the past. Yet, while, in our prejudice, we speak of Greece, Rome and India as all past and dead, what was once beautiful and good in them survives in the countries in which it took its birth, however dimmed and obscured by evil agencies, and lives as a mighty force in the countries of its adoption. There is one eternal cause, great and beneficent, towards which tend, irresistibly, all human movements, during successive ages. "Nothing beautiful and good perishes in the world; neither liberty, poetry, virtue, nor justice. And when a passing cloud ever and anon renders them invisible to the human eye, when they are momentarily eclipsed, and faithless mortals are thus encouraged in the belief that they have perished, they soon after are beheld again, rekindled and bright, as if they were as immortal as the human souls which they ennoble."

Is it true, then, that "India is all past, and has no future," while the true, the good, the beautiful in her yet live, and while hundreds of thousands of her sons, whose number will soon grow into millions, see only in the past a grand and glorious vision, which, aided and strengthened by the light of the present, will, they sanguinely hope and trust, lead them to a grand future? These aspirations, this longing after progress, is a living and veritable force, which has to be taken into account when we take upon ourselves to predict that she has no future. Evil agencies, the efforts of all the evil passions, if the present aspirations last, will be but infinitesimal obstacles, which will soon be drowned in the great progressive streams. Already these aspirations are at work.

We have amongst us, at the present day, (1) the Hindu Revivalists; (2) the Hindu iconoclast Occidentalists; (3) the Provincialists; (4) the Mahomedan Nationalists; the European and Eurasian Defence Associationists; the Eurasian Associationists; the Armenian Associationists; (5) the Indian Nationalists, each and all engaged, according to their respective lights, in promoting progress in India, for separate communities, or for India as a whole. The procedure may be different in each case; but in all it tends in the same direction. There may be at the present date *apparent* conflict of interests, or even selfishness, and in that selfishness an utter obliviousness, nay obstruction, of the progress of India as a whole; but who will deny that, in trying to improve the parts, one and all are contributing to the improvement of the whole? The Indians of the future are destined to grow out of these differentiations, and the most profound thinker of the age somewhere beautifully says: "In the social organism, as in the individual organism, differentiations cease only with that completion of the type which marks maturity and precedes decay."

(1) The Hindu Revivalists think of reproducing the glorious *India* of the past; but, though they are useful at the present day, not only as a progressive factor,—for there is no gainsaying the fact that, if we could reproduce the India of the Sixth century of the Christian era, the day when the nine *gems*

adorned the glorious Court of Vicramaditya with poetry, science and art which even now excite the admiration of the world, it would bring India and her people nearer to the Nineteenth century than they are at present, but also as a reactionary movement to that of the Hindu iconoclast Occidentalists, who will next come under review, they are soon destined to find that the ideal of the past is far below that of the Nineteenth century. Again, what part of the past are they to reproduce? The Hindus of the day of Vicramajeet did not stand exactly where they were in the days of the Vedas, nor did the Hindus of the Puranic period stand where they were in the days of Vicramajeet.

The Revivalists forget that no reproduction of the *India of the past* is possible unless all the conditions under which India then existed, can be restored—India living by herself alone, unconnected with the rest of the world; her people growing their own food in their fertile and virgin soil, enough to spare and bestow on others; her people manufacturing their own clothes in their own looms, with but few wants which they themselves could not supply—the classes above free from the Nineteenth-century struggle for bread, with ample leisure to think and to produce; *cowries* instead of silver coins; prices cheap and wants few. What prevents our revivalists from preserving a social type which is not yet dead, though fast dying? "The Pundits who used to teach in the *toles*—टोल—never cared for the rewards of this world. They loved their work for the sake of their work. They loved their pupils as their children. No fees were ever charged, and in many cases the pupils were housed and fed by the teachers. The example of the self-sacrificing Pundits, whose care was only the welfare of their pupils, infected their household. No sacrifice was considered sacrifice by them or by theirs, when undertaken for this pious and meritorious motive. The Pundits used to have in return, the love and the veneration of their pupils, and the respect of the community they lived in. Things have now changed a good deal even in our indigenous *toles*, टोल, and in our English schools they are nowhere. Even the descendants of these very Pundits, though they now receive better pay than the precarious income their ancestors earned by the good-will of the community in which they lived, find the department of education not at all attractive. They have forgotten the self-sacrificing spirit of their ancestors, and it is partially owing to this, that they do not enjoy the love and veneration of their pupils. Is it possible to revive the old Hindu spirit in our teachers of the day? We are afraid not. The reasons which make a revival of this sort impossible, are to be found in the social and economic changes that have come around us."

Again, the Revivalists have to take account of the causes which have brought about the present degenerate condition of the Hindus. Why did not the progress achieved at the date of Vicramajeet last? What contributed to the decay of the Hindus? The answer is short; there was no Indian Nation at the date of Vicramajeet, or at any period of past Indian history. The causes which are now happily tending to the growth of an Indian Nation were then non-existent.

To the Revivalists, patriots as they are, we say that they must not forget that the India of to-day is not the country of the Hindus alone. It is as much the country of the 40 millions of Mahomedans as of the 210 millions of Hindus; and it is also the country of the Europeans, Eurasians, Armenians, Jews and Parsis—important classes, though few in numbers. The foreign element was not wanting in the India of the past; but the genius of our ancestors, by fictions which they alone knew how to invent, to suit all occasions, had been receiving within their systems the Greeks, the Bactrians, and, lastly, even after the time of Vicramajeet, and only 200 or 300 years before the invasion of Mahmud of Ghor, foreigners from the West, giving them the proud position of the Rajputs of the present day. If with the revival of ancient Hindu glory, our Revivalists could, as our ancestors did of old, incorporate with our system the various foreign elements, Musalmans, Christians, Jews and Parsis, they would, no doubt, find themselves at one with the Indian Nationalists; but as the days of fiction have almost passed; they will have to take a new departure, and evolve out of the past, a future unfettered by the traditionary usages and practices of the dead past, a future suited to the genius of their race, in consonance with the usages and practices of others with whom they are now in contact. When that departure shall have been made, which we hope it soon will be, then but little distinction will remain between them and the Indian Nationalists

(2). The usefulness of the class whom we have designated Hindu iconoclast Occidentalists—we mean no disrespect in applying the term to a body of earnest workers for whom we have profound esteem —has been very great, and their aim has always been progress in every direction, and progress for India as a whole. They were the earliest, and we may say the first natural product of the contact of India with the material civilization of the West; but the early zeal with which they proceeded to break up everything existent in this country, and to substitute in its stead, without much discrimination, imitations of the West, soon excited a revulsion of feeling in their own countrymen, and the reaction of the revivalists showed that their procedure was wrong, and that their usefulness would be ephemeral. Their diminished number proves that this prognostication was not unjust, and, as things are now more correctly understood than they were only a few years ago, they are already amalgamating, almost as a class, with the Indian Nationalists, with whom they have always agreed in their aims.

(3). It was but natural that people, before they could think of India as a whole, should begin to think of its individual parts—the Bengalis of Bengal, the Mahrattas of Maharastra, and the Madrasis of Madras. There would thus spring up a certain amount of provincial jealousy, and this has been made much of so long as it served the purpose of those who preach, as sound policy, the disintegration of India into parts. Happily, so far as the Hindus are concerned, the days of provincial jealousy have vanished before the bright vision of an Indian nationality; and any endeavour to revive it must meet with an ignominious failure. The Bengali is now a brother to the Mahratta, the Punjabi to the Madrasi; and, while each is doing his best to advance with his immediate environment, and to look to the interests of his own province, the interests of the province have already come to be regarded as subordinate to those of India as a whole.

There has not been a greater change in anything else, perhaps, than in this. Five years ago,* before the national aspirations had yet been properly defined, when Mr. Cotton, in his admirable work, "*New India*," following in the wake of Mr. Bright, suggested provincial autonomy, with Hindu predominance in some parts, and Mahomedan in others, and separate and distinct settlements for Europeans, and others bearing European names, all federated

* This was written in 1890.

together under a central Government, the scheme met with universal applause amongst the educated Hindus in all parts of India. But the scheme no longer satisfies the popular and national aspirations. We may show, hereafter, why this is so. At present we bring forward this to show how provincialism, in the narrowest sense, has died out.

(4). The Mahomedan Nationalists, and the rest, in so far as they are trying to better the condition of their respective classes, are working for the common good of India; for, as we have said, the advancement of all the parts means the advancement of the whole. They work in this matter on the same lines as those who work for India as a whole, with a sanguine hope of a grand future. But it is urged that there is a conflict of interests, and some individuals of these communities argue, that, with due regard to the interests of their respective classes, they are bound to obstruct measures calculated to promote the common good of India. These latter among the Mahomedans speak of a "Mahomedan Nation," and we therefore designate them Mahomedan Nationalists. The two points we propose to examine in this connection are, (1) whether there is any real conflict of interests; (2), whether there is "a Mahomedan Nation" in India.

Of the 33 millions of Mahomedans in British India,* there are 19 millions or thereabouts in Bengal, about

* Taken from the census figures of 1882-83.

10 millions in Behar, the United Provinces and the Punjab, and about 4 millions in all the rest of India. The two principal centres therefore are, (1) Bengal; (2) the United Provinces, Behar and the Punjab. It will be found that the condition of the Mahomedans differs essentially in these two centres. Of the 19 millions of Mahomedans in Bengal, not more than 25,000 belong to what is known in Bengal as the *Bhadralog* class. The remainder are agriculturists, day labourers, and petty artizans, tailors and domestic servants. These were originally Hindus of the *jal-achal* class, who were converted to Mahomedanism. As a class, they are the most prosperous tenantry in India, and their condition, instead of deteriorating, as that of Mahomedans throughout India is ordinarily supposed to be, is daily improving. They were never anything more than agriculturists, and at no period of their history either government servants, government soldiers, or zemindars, much less conquerors of India, or even followers of the Mahomedan conquerors. They are born of the country, speak the Bengali language, write the Bengali character, dress like Bengalis, eat almost the same food as Bengalis, and, except as to matters of religion, resemble in all respects any other Bengali ryot. They are not the men who are said to be animated by traditionary pride of race, as conquerors, in relation to the Bengali-Hindus. Most of them are the tenants of Bengali-Hindu zemindars, and

the neighbours and friends of Bengali-Hindu ryots. *Dada*, *chacha*, *mama* are the endearing terms of relationship the Hindu and Musalman, Bengali ryots employ in addressing each other. Even in matters of religion, the *Ram* of the one is the *Rahim* of the other, and one of the most popular religious versifiers on the attributes of the Hindu goddess *Kali*, was a Mahomedan whose songs are sung by peasants of all classes. The few Mahomedan shrines in Bengal are always visited by Hindus with offerings, and on the occasion of any undertaking, especially a boat journey, the *Ghazi sirni* (one pice worth of sweets) is always, as a rule, offered by ryots, Hindus and Mahomedans alike, to the *Ghazi* (Mahomedan saint). The boatmen, Hindu and Mahomedan, on entering or crossing a river, shout "पाँच पीर बदार बदीर" "Panch Pir Bodour, Bodour." *

Bengal has never known a Mohurrum outbreak. There is not, indeed, much Mohurrum except in the large towns of Calcutta, Dacca and Murshidabad. Most of the converts are Sunnis; but beyond the *Kalma*, their knowledge of Mahomedan theology is *nil*. Only once in the history of their quiet life was there a fanatical outbreak—the Ferazi revival, shortly before the Mutiny; but those who care to read the proceedings of a celebrated trial at Faridpur, in which Dudu Mia, the Ferazi leader and his followers,

* Invocations to the Mahomedan Saint Bodour-ul-Alum.

were charged with larceny and rioting attended with culpable homicide, &c., will find that the outbreak originated in the oppression of the Mahomedan tenantry by certain zemindars and European Indigo-planters—the earliest agrarian disturbance in Bengal, though it subsequently found vent in a fanatical zeal on the part of Musalmans against Kafirs of all classes. Since then the Mollahs have been going about, but they have not yet succeeded in instructing their disciples beyond the most rudimentary points of the faith, and certainly have not been able to infect the general body of the Mahomedan peasantry with their fanatical zeal.

We thus see that 18,975,000 of the Mahomedans, out of the 19 millions, *i.e.*, 99·9 per cent. of that body, instead of deteriorating, are improving day by day as prosperous agriculturists. The schools are open to them as to others; but it is doubtful whether any of them would choose to substitute the pen for the plough, or whether, if they were to choose, they would gain by entering the lists with the *Bhadralog* (Mahomedans and Hindus) for petty clerkships and mohurirships in our courts and offices. Their natural leaders, as we have said, are their zemindars and educated men in their neighbourhood, in 99 cases Hindus, to whom they resort for advice and assistance in all difficult matters.

The next question is whether the remaining 25,000 have deteriorated, and whether they are comparatively more backward than the Hindus. A comparison is made between 25 millions of Hindus in Bengal and 19 millions of Musalmans; our Civil Lists and University Calendars are ransacked for the purpose, and when by such a comparison it is found that the Musalman percentage is small, it is concluded that there is deterioration and backwardness. But to view the subject in this way is to start with a false premise. The comparison should really be made between 25,000 Musalmans and 5 million Hindu *Bhadralog*, and the result of such a comparison will show that, neither as regards offices, nor as regards University degrees, is there any backwardness whatever on the part of the Bengali Musalmans of the *Bhadralog* class.

Let us now examine the case of the Mahomedans of Behar, the United Provinces and the Punjab. The upper stratum is, no doubt, larger than in Bengal, but not in any way equal to the *Bhadralog* class of the Hindus. For instance, in Behar the upper stratum of Hindu society, comprising the castes of Brahmins, Rajputs, Babhans, Kshettris and Kayesthas, includes a population of upwards of 3 millions out of 18 millions, or the entire Hindu population of the province, while the corresponding class amongst the Mahomedans does not exceed 150,000 out of 3 millions, and out of this 150,000, a very large number, comprising the entire Mahomedan population of a respectable order in an inportant centre, were, a few generations back, Hindus. In the United Provinces and the Punjab the case, we believe, is slightly better; but, except on occasions of fanatical outbreaks in towns, the lower stratum of the Mahomedan population follow the lead of their Hindu zemindars and other leading men amongst the Hindus, as much as they follow the lead of Mahomedans; they speak the same language as the corresponding classes amongst the Hindus, write the same character, dress alike, and share alike the ills to which the labouring classes in the Upper Provinces are subject. Riots between neighbouring zemindars, or neighbouring villages, mostly for rights of irrigation, are very common in Behar, and Hindu and Mahomedan ryots of one village, or tenants of one zemindar, fight against the Hindu and Mahomedan ryots of another village or another zemindar. If the criminal reports are searched, not a single case of these riots will be found in which the Mahomedans fight the Hindus as Hindus. In the village economy, the capacities of different men, or different classes of men, are well understood by Hindus and Mahomedans alike. The Patwary is always a Kayestha, and never a Musalman: the Gomastha is either a Rajput or a Mahomedan. The city of Patna is one of the towns in India where the Mohurrum is celebrated with much *eclât*. We are told, by the Mahomedans themselves that, in this respect, it now ranks above all other towns, not even Lucknow excepted.

If any one will watch the proceedings on the *Pallam* day (the last burial day of the Tazia) from the Darga in the city of Patna, he will find that more than five-sixths of the stream of people who wend their way from all sides of the town to this centre, are Hindus, calling *Hasan! Hosain!* and beating their breasts, and carrying the Mohurrum trophies like any ordinary *Shiah*. Indeed, a large proportion of the Tazias are made and taken in procession at the expense of the Hindus, and the most splendid one, which comes on at the end (*Chamoondaria*), belongs as much to the Hindus as to the Mahomedans of the city Chowk. These processions go on from year to year peaceably and harmoniously, unless it be for a merry fight between one *Akhra* and another, in which case it is not a fight of Hindus and Musalmans for their respective religions, but of one portion of the town against another, in honor of the greatness of their respective Tazias, or an expression of their local rivalry. We hear much of the Mohurrum outbreaks which are occasional and rare, but we do not ordinarily hear how, from year to year, the Mohurrum peaceably passes off as a national festival of the Hindus and Mahomedans alike in most of the towns of Upper India. It is true that the lower stratum of Mahomedan society in Behar, the United Provinces, and the Punjab is not so prosperous as the corresponding classes in Bengal, but even in that matter, in their one meal and the hardness of their penurious life, they are being welded with the correspond-ing classes of the Hindus into one mass, and few in this country understand what is meant when a distinct nationality is claimed for them along with their betters.

As for their betters, forming the upper stratum of Mahomedan society, and comprising (we chose to err on the wrong side) half a million out of ten millions, the Mahomedans, like the Hindus of the upper classes, are zemindars, Government servants, professional men, or merchants and trades-people of the better sort.

The immediate necessity in the case of zemindars, both Hindu and Mahomedan, not being pressing, they did not take advantage of the educational opportunities afforded to all classes by the Government; but this conduct of theirs was short-sighted, and has proved to some extent disastrous in both cases, though more so in the case of the Mahomedans than the Hindus; for the law of inheritance went on inexorably distributing the heritages from generation to generation, in smaller and smaller shares, amongst the former than amongst the latter. As for the other classes, it is extremely doubtful whether, having regard to their number, the *Bhadralog* class amongst the Mahomedans are at a disadvantage, as compared with the Hindus of the corresponding class: we believe more lucrative appointments under Government are now held by Mahomedans in the

(5.) The Indian Nationalists, who now, happily, include in their ranks almost all the educated Hindus, a very large proportion of educated Mahomedans, and a number of domiciled Europeans, Eurasians, Parsis, and members of other races of India, believe that India is not altogether dead, but has before her a grand future. They rejoice to find the germs of a national growth, and sanguinely hope to foster such growth. Each in his own section strives to educate and to bring up his community to a common national standard, wiping off angularities where such exist—angularities which prevent the common national growth,—but, at the same time, without in the least trying to do violence to, but on the contrary endeavouring to conserve such differentiations in the different sections of the common body as are peculiar to them. With this programme, progress in all directions is their motto ; and, though they have met in an Indian National Congress for the last five years simply to discuss some of the most interesting political questions affecting India as a whole in which all are interested, and a smaller portion of the Hindu delegates in a Social Conference, it is, we hope, now understood by friends and foes, that their programme is as broad as the growth and progress of an Indian nation in every direction —social, moral and political.

But it is asked—Where is this Indian nation ? We shall answer this question by bringing forward a historical parallel.

The Roman Empire, composed mainly of towns, and deficient in a rural population, fell, in spite of its mightiness and grandeur, before the inroads of the barbarians, and the progress of centuries was arrested. The barbarians succeeded, not through the united efforts of a body politic, but through the personal greatness of some of their chiefs in founding such great empires as that of Charlemagne. But the Empire of Charlemagne fell, and fell before it was ripe, before fresh inroads of barbarians. Europe, the Empire of Charlemagne included, became divided into feudal units, and it was only the occurrence of one great event which primarily brought about the formation of the European nations. The phenomena in India have not been exactly similar, but you will find events for events, in close sequence.

It was not here a great Empire, like that of Rome, weakened and enervated by causes which need not here be recapitulated, that fell, but petty states into which the India of the day was divided, corresponding to the cities of the Great Roman Empire, *minus* the central government, which, at the end, in the case of the Roman Empire, had come to be a word of derision. These petty kingdoms fell before a Mahomedan invasion, and not exactly a barbarian inroad; for the Mahomedan invaders of India had a civilization of their own, though inferior to that of the conquered Hindus. Take Akbar for Charlemagne, and you will find another part of the parallel comthe most anciently civilized of the four quarters of the globe. They began to study the arts, creeds, and idioms of its inhabitants. The world seemed to open on the side of the East."

On the same subject another writer says—"Such, in my opinion, were the great and true effects of the Crusades: on one side, the extension of ideas, the enfranchisement of mind; on the other, the aggrandizement of existences, and a large sphere opened to activity of all kinds—they produced at once a greater degree of individual liberty and of political unity. They aided the independence of men, and the centralization of society. Much has been asked as to the means of civilization which they directly imported from the East; it has been said that the chief portion of the great discoveries which, in the fourteenth and fifteenth centuries called forth the deep development of European civilization—the compass, printing, and gunpowder,—were known in the East, and that the Crusaders may have brought them thence. This, to a certain point is true. But some of these assertions are disputable. That which is not, is the influence and the general effect of the Crusades upon the mind on the one hand, and upon society on the other. They drew European society from a very straitened track, and led it into new and infinitely more extensive paths; they commenced that transformation of the various elements of European society into governments and peoples, which is the character of modern civilization."

In almost the same words may be described the effect of the event in India which has again brought the West and the East into contact more intimately than the Crusades ever did. The far-reaching effects of this closer relationship, we shall have occasion to touch upon hereafter.

Now we hope to be permitted to answer the question—"Where is this Indian Nation?" by putting another question—Where was the French Nation before the 12th century? Let us hear the testimony of one of the greatest of French historians: "The races, Gauls, Romans, Gallo-Romans, Franks, Gallo-Franks were profoundly different, and even hostile; the laws, traditions, manners, languages likewise differed and conflicted; situations, social relations, had neither generality nor fixedness."

Now, France had not the ancient civilization of India in the background, and the modern progress of the world in the foreground, to look to at the time when, under circumstances almost exactly similar, she came to grow into a nation, to become, in the course of few centuries, the foremost nation in the world.

It will not be denied that political unity serves as much to foster the growth of a nation as moral unity. The external, visible unity—the unity of name and government—is one of the most important elements in the idea of a nation. Professor Seeley says, "Nationality is compounded of several ele-

of the world's progress, as in it has met all the hereditary wealth of mankind, moral and intellectual, of all past times. The practical here meets the subtle and the metaphysical, and the contact must tend to the benefit of both. Professor Seeley says: "The greatness of modern, as compared with mediæval or ancient civilization, is, that it possesses a larger stock of demonstrated truths, and therefore infinitely more of practical power." If India were in a state of isolation from modern Europe, it might be just possible for the poetical and mystic Indians to be disposed to despise demonstrated truth, with the power it brings. They might choose to call it shallow, and to sneer at its practical triumphs, while revelling for their own part in reveries and in the luxuries of unbounded speculation; but a practical sense of want, a consciousness that if they were to exist even for the subtle and metaphysical, they could only exist, in the present circumstances, under different conditions, intervenes, and brings them face to face with the actual realities of life. This sense of want, this consciousness that in the actual realities of life they have been outstripped by the practical people of Europe, is now almost universal among the Indians, and the feeling is making them one. Any attempt to take advantage of the practical truths demonstrated, in whatever part of India, and by Indian people of any denomination, pleases the whole of India. There is an almost universal desire not to be dependent on others for all the necessities of life. In Bengal they have a song which is even now sung by their *Jatrawallas*, boatmen, and other common people, describing this national want, and consequent poverty, and the people's feelings regarding it.

Feelings like this must make a nation—and it is in this that the European section of the community will first blend with the Hindu and the Musalman, to form a nation. The European, if he does not degenerate, must bring to India the practical. Already he is, in many cases, developing the resources of the country, and his example is being imitated by Indians of other denominations in many useful walks of life. We have our mill-owners, Indigo-planters and tea-planters, &c. The European portion of the community resent more keenly than the other Indians (Hindus and Musulmans) any measures which spring from a desire to satisfy the greed of capitalists or mill-owners in England at the expense of native Indian manufactures and trade. And if we are permitted here to enter into the domain of speculation, we may predict that, with her vast resources as a great agricultural country, India is destined soon to regain her position as a great manufacturing country, which she held before the days of machines, and peacefully to re-conquer the world again; solving in that re-conquest two of the knotty questions pertaining to labour in the present day (the working-man's difficulty)

in the vernacular, or in Hindi. If the five Universities of India were conjointly to set about the task, it would not be at all difficult; and success in it will be attended by this merit that, wherever a term has to be coined in the vernaculars,—and many terms will have to be coined,—it will come from a common mint, with the imprimatur of all the Universities attached to it The Calcutta University has frittered away, from year to year, a portion of the splendid endowments in its gift, but yet there are no scientific works, no high mathematical works, no good historical works in Bengali, or, for the matter of that, in any of the vernaculars of India. The growth of modern Indian literature, history, science, mathematics and philosophy should have, as its basis, translations from European languages; and the foundation once laid, with the materials ready and at command—the accumulated stores of centuries of European civilization only waiting to be laid down—the superstructure, which, to be beautiful, should be indigenous, must come in time. We hear of too much cramming now-a-days, but if our Universities were to teach our boys their geography, their history, their mathematics, their philosophy, their science, in their own vernaculars, much cramming would be avoided, and a great deal of precious time saved.

We leave the subject of the growth of vernacular literature to our authors, and we do not extend to them the least amount of protection. Their productions do not sell, not because none of them write well, but because there is no reading public, and vernacular literature is at a discount with our young men. Yet, amidst such discouragements, Bengal at least has, within the last thirty years, produced authors whose reputation, actually confined to Bengal, should have been Indian. Some of our young authors who have made literature their profession, finding Bengali unprofitable, have taken to translating Sanscrit works into English. It is admirable work, no doubt, but we leave it as a suggestion, whether our authors, both to acquire an Indian reputation, and to make their literature pay, would not do well to write in Hindi. The language of Tulsidas is now almost universally understood throughout India, and, from days earlier than those of Bharat Chandra, the language in which Tulsidas wrote, has been written with all its idioms, and its sweet diction, and with masterly skill, by our Bengali authors, when they have attempted it. The reason for this is clear. The Bengali has branched out from the Hindi within the last 300 years. The poetry of Kabikankun, Vidiapati and Govind Das might, with slight changes, be published as Hindi works, and an edition of "Chaitanya Charitra Mitra" might be published in Hindi, without any change at all. The differentiation, indeed, of Hindi and Bengali is only clearly discernible in the last century, and it is unhappily the aim of our modern Bengali authors to make it more marked. In this matter, their action has been the same as that of our paternal Government, which has raised the Assamese to the rank of a distinct language, and which, without pronouncing any definite policy, has encouraged the publication of seven Grammars of seven provincial dialects of the Hindi language, with provincialism not more marked than the Bengali of the several districts of Bengal. Hindi is now the language of the courts in the Punjab, the United Provinces, and, thanks to the statesmanship of Sir George Campbell, in Behar. It should be the language of the courts in the Central Provinces; and, as the terms in use in the courts are almost the same throughout India, it might with advantage be extended to those of Bengal, Guzerat and Maharastra. The Bengalis and Maharattas would be very unreasonable, indeed, if they were to resist the change.

(5.) Geographical difficulties have hitherto, to a great extent, retarded the growth of a United India, and favoured provincialism. These difficulties have now been happily swept away. Distances have been annihilated by railways and telegraphs. "I am a part of what I see," sings the poet; and a common Government, with its peace and security, its railways and steamers, connecting, as it does, the most distant parts of India with one another, and rendering travelling convenient and easy, makes a solidarity of Indian customs and manners possible. The Indian

National Congress renders an important service in this respect; and, when the people of Bengal and the North-Western Provinces see Hindu females of respectable families of Bombay and Madras appearing before the public, the wives of Indian Brahmin Judges, and Indian Brahmin councillors, coming to see the proceedings of the Congress, and taking part, not from behind the *purdah*, in the public receptions of the Congress delegates, they cannot, however conservative they may be in their feelings with respect to the seclusion of women, regard these public appearances as un-Hindu; and when, on returning home, they speak of these matters from personal observation, a new interest is created and a new way opened for reform.

When, in the same way, the Bengalis see the Kashmiri Brahmin taking food brought for him by a Musalman, and using water fetched in his *mussuck*, even the most rigid conservatives among them cannot condemn the action and practices of our more zealous reformers in the same style as before.

The home-staying Bengali regards *Sanghai* marriages as an entirely Mahomedan custom, and when he comes to know that widow marriage prevails, to a large extent, amongst the Hindu people of India, he ceases to condemn it as un-Hindu.

Marriage at ages which we considered proper for marriage in all societies, is customary in Hindu society in some parts of India, and even love marriages, in Indian forms, are not quite out of rule. Homogeneity of Hindu practice in different parts of India would bring about all that the most ardent reformers desire. In this respect there is no need for the importation of foreign articles till all our indigenous sources have been exhausted.

Already something like a homogeneity is growing up in the matter of dress; and amongst the divergences of dresses, conspicuously in the head-dress, observable in an assembly from all parts of India, as in the Indian National Congress, even a casual observer must mark that, from year to year, uniformity is growing, and the time is not far distant when the Indian national dress for males will come to consist of a pair of trousers, a long Parsi coat, and a light *pugri* of the sort which made our friend, the Hon'ble Sobramania Ayyar, of Madras, look so decent and graceful in the Calcutta Congress of 1886.

The few Indian ladies who presented themselves at the Congress as delegates from different parts of India were, colour apart, dressed almost all alike. There can hardly be a better dress or one more suited to the Indian climate, for use at home, than that now in vogue almost throughout India,—a *dhoti* and shirt for males, and a *sari* and jacket for females.

The Indian wardrobe has always been very simple, and we hope it will remain so for all time to come.

These are the circumstances which are contributing to the growth of an Indian Nation; but there are certain circumstances which are pointed out as bars to that growth. These are:—1st, the want of a common religion; 2nd, the want of a common language; 3rd, the Hindu caste system; 4th, the conflict of interests of the different sections of the community.

With reference to the first we have shown that the obstacle is more apparent than real; that the binding force of creeds has been much exaggerated, and that the tie which binds all good men and true to one another, irrespective of creeds, is too often lost sight of.

With regard to the second: we have shown that, though its function is only temporary, the English language, which is being spoken by a larger and larger number of Indian people from year to year, serves as a common vehicle of speech, at least for the representative classes of the Indian population. Except in Bengal, the Hindi, or rather the hybrid Urdu, is the language of the Mahomedan population of India, as also of the Hindu population inhabiting more than half of India; while in the lesser half, it is understood without any difficulty whatever. The hybrid Urdu does not take much time to change into the purer Hindi: witness the change introduced by Sir George Campbell in the language of the courts in Behar.

The third point requires a somewhat more lengthened examination. The author of "*Positive Philosophy*" said:—

"No institution has ever shewn itself more adapted to honour ability of various kinds than this polytheistic organization, which often exalted into apotheosis its. commemorations of eminent inventors, who were offered to the adoration of their respective castes. In a social view, the virtues of the system are not less conspicuous. Politically, its chief attribute was stability. All precautions against attack from within and from without were most energetically instituted. . . . . . . As to the influence on morals, this system was favourable to personal morality, and yet more to domestic; for the spirit of caste was a mere extension of the family spirit. . . . As to social morals, the system was evidently favourable to respect for age and homage to ancestors. The sentiment of patriotism did not as yet transcend love of caste, which, narrow as its appears to us, was a necessary preparation for the higher attachment."

On the other hand, in his work on "*Ancient Civilization in India*," Mr. R. C. Dutt sees in the institution of the caste system the cause of the downfal' of India. What is there in it which the foreigner, the greatest philosopher of this or of any age, admires, and which an Indian thus condemns. We have analyzed caste, and shown that there is no rigidity, no inflexibility about it; that its requirements have changed from time to time, and that very soon, its only requirement will come to be "not to marry outside the caste." We have shown what cautious changes are possible even here, and what changes, if introduced, would be popular. Will this interdict of marriages retard the growth of an Indian Nation? We believe not. We do not see all angularities wiped out even in a fullgrown nation; perhaps, in some cases, inequalities grow, and are hourly growing—these inequalities are inequalities of wealth and power. They give rise to distinctions between man and man, and this, in a marked manner, in such free countries as England, where all men are politically equal. There is the plebeian hatred and the patrician pride; and not that feeling of subordination, which the hierarchy of caste engenders, and which keeps these disintegrating feelings in check where it exists. It is very probable that in India caste, at least amongst the Aryan settlers themselves, originated in the same sort of distinction between man and man which the philosophers saw in the "*New Atlantis*," or in "*Utopia*." At least we have an authentic record that what was a Utopian dream in Europe was practically attempted in India by one of her late kings, (Ballal Sen). But it was a dream in Europe and a failure in India. The failure, not Ballal Sen's, but of the earliest unrecorded ones of the series, together, of course, with other causes too many to enumerate in this place, has left us the hereditary caste system. That system is primarily supposed to be based on birth and hereditary occupation; but hereditary occupation no longer exists, and there is nothing in the nature of things to prevent a man, plebeian born, from rising as high in the social scale, in the European sense, as he can. Examples of this, under the benign British Government, are numerous; but at no time, perhaps, was there anything like an interdict to their rising in this sense. All castes afford authentic instances of the rise of some of their individual members, dating from the remotest times.

Caste divisions now spring only from birth; and who will not prize them as conducing to the levelling and wiping out of distinctions between man and man, grounded on the possession of wealth or power. It is only lately that the lady Superintendent of the Bethune School has, by her writing in the newspapers, in which she seeks to draw a distinction between the girl students under her charge, as belonging to the upper, middle, and lower classes of the Indian people, according to the means of their parents or guardians, excited the ire, amongst others, of a gentleman who is a Brahmo, though originally a high caste Brahmin, and who has done more than any one else to do away with the fetters of caste, and of another who is an Indian Christian. Both these gentlemen appeal to birth as the standard of division in India, and take the lady to task for trying to import occidental distinctions which do not exist in the Indian system. Our Mahomedan brethren appeal to the same principle, and Indian Christians of the *Bhadralog* class can never be persuaded to mix in marriage with Christians who were not *Bhadralog.* It is an instinctive admission that of the two, birth, or supposed birth, is a better regulating principle of division between man and man, than the distinction founded mainly on wealth or power. In a political point of view, we have shown that the one is a greater disintegrating factor than the other.

There is a reflected glory in a long list of ancestors, and, in India, prince and peasant can alike trace their ancestry, in an unbroken series, to the remotest past. Caste alone conserves this unbroken list. There is again, an *esprit de corps,* a love of caste, which, "narrow as it appears to us, is a necessary preparation for the higher attachment" to one's own country and its people. It is like the provincialism to which we referred at the beginning of this chapter, subsidiary, but by no means antagonistic, to Indian nationalism. In countries where the birth principle does not prevail, nothing we suppose, is more common than for a pastor's daughter to be a governess, or in the second generation, for the daughter's daughter to be a maidservant. The cousin of a man rolling in wealth is not uncommonly found discharging service not befitting his rank, and in many cases his descendants sink never to rise again. Such things were impossible in India a few years ago, and are impossible even now. Here a man reduced to abject poverty is preserved by the spirit of his caste. Once, in the course of conversation with the present writer, a missionary gentleman—one of those types whom all classes respect—expressed his wonder that the undergraduate of our Universities, instead of seeking employment as a clerk on ten rupees in a mercantile office, or elsewhere, does not become head khansamah in some big Chowringhee-house. The reason given then stands good now, and we hope will stand good for all time to come. He cannot forget, if a *Bhadralog*, that he is a *Bhadralog* born, and, though reduced to want, he choses to remain a *Bhadralog*. With this feeling in him, and in all coming after him, he, his children, or his remoter descendants, must rise to-morrow, or at a more distant date, if they are down in the world to-day. Even if he be the poorest of the poor, the other people of his caste are bound to pay him the same consideration as they previously paid him or his family. If he is their equal, they must ask him to their caste dinners, to all their caste meetings, and in all cases, the rich being few, they, the rich, under the rules of caste, must accept him and his for marriage-connections as well.

But the greatest service which caste, or rather its rigid interdict of marriages, has done, is this; it has served to preserve the Hindu name under a foreign yoke. It did not allow India to be Musalmanised. The interdict, in its most rigid form, dates only from a time when India came to be overrun by foreigners. The early conquerors of India had Aryanised India by conquest, marriages, conversion, and colonization. The "*Ramayan*" begins with the story of "Risha Sringa," an Arya Brahmin, who is lured away from his father to some kingdom, south-east of the Nerbudda, for marriage with the daughter of the Raja, evidently a non-Aryan. The marriage is celebrated with *éclat*, and when the irate father comes to claim his son, he is appeased by seeing beautiful towns erected all along his way, and passing for towns of his son, till then as beggarly as he.

The marriage of Jaratkaru, sister of the non-Aryan Nags of the forest, with Jaratkaru Rishi, the Aryan, is another instance. There are like cases all the world over, and recurring at all times of its history. They show how eager are the weaker people to enter into marriage alliances with the stronger conquerors, and assimilate themselves with them. The non-Aryans lost their distinct existence, as the Britons lost theirs, and as many other races in Europe and Asia lost theirs. If the Hindus could, without incurring the strong censure of their people which loss of caste implies, marry into the conquering race they also would do so, and their distinct existence as a people would have by this time entirely gone. Should we, therefore, be in a hurry to do away with this interdict, which has served to preserve us as a distinct people amidst all our adversities, so long as we are what we are? We have indicated how far a slow progress, a relaxation of a rigid rule, is possible. Perhaps, in time, the Hindus will come to assimilate themselves to the ancient practice indicated in the Shastras, and there will be no interdict to marriages between Hindus and Hindus in an *anulom* form. But this social interdict, which we have shown practically means nothing, is no bar to the political union of the Hindus, as a people with other races who now inhabit India.

As to the fourth point. We have already shown that there is in reality no conflict of interests between the different races of India. The cry which is now and then raised, that, if the Hindus had a strong voice in our legislative councils, they would stop the killing of kine by a legislative enactment, is too silly to deserve consideration; and, except the one point sought to be touched by the Ilbert Bill, one can scarcely conceive of any other instance of conflict of interests between race and race in India which could engage the attention of our legislative councils. In all other respects, the same laws govern India, the same taxes are levied from all around, and if a screw gets loose, anywhere, it effects A, as well as B and C. A higher state of education will clear up obscurer visions, and again we say—evil agencies, the efforts of all the evil passions, if the present aspirations last, will be but atomic obstacles, which will be drowned in the great progressive streams.

We have sufficiently indicated what the basal conditions of Indian Nationalism are; 1st. Appreciation of the blessings of a common Government; 2nd. Toleration for all kinds of religious views—and we are glad that at least four-fifths of the population of India are prepared by their religious teachings to accept this as a condition of union; 3rd. Subordination of the parts to the whole. The Hindu family system,—nay, the despised caste system—is, in this connection, an aid and not an obstacle; 4th. An honest desire for an indigenous growth, free from all foreign imitations—the experience of the earliest Aryan settlers in India being taken as a guide for the solution of knotty questions of social ethics in relation to the climatic condition of the country.

There is one more point and we have done. Professor Seeley, after examining the question whether the English conquered India, and answering it in the negative, observes that England holds India because there is no Indian nation, and then proceeds to say:—"A population that rebels, is a population that is looking up, that has begun to hope and to feel its strength. But if such a rising took place, it would be put down by the Native soldiery, so long as they have not learnt to feel themselves brothers to Hindus, and foreigners to the Englishman that commands them. But on the other hand, if this feeling ever does spring up, if

India does begin to breathe as a single national whole—and our own rule is perhaps doing more than ever was done by former Governments to make this possible—then no such explosion of despair, even if there were cause for it, would be needed." The Professor would not have, perhaps, thought that the growth of the feeling of nationality in India would be immediately followed by a desire on the part of the Indians to separate India from England, if the remedies which he suggests for preventing such a desire, and for securing a permanent connection between England and her colonies, were applicable to the case of India: that is, in other words, if India could be included in what he calls "Greater Britain," and if the federal system which he recommends for adoption in relation to the colonies could be extended to India. Nowhere is this scheme of federalization fully defined; but we gather that it is something like this: each colony having a Parliament to look to its internal affairs, with a Government responsible to its own Parliament, and a central body of representatives of "Greater Britain," sitting in England, entrusted with the duty of looking to its common defence from external foes.

Let there be no misunderstanding on the point: the present aspirations enunciated in the Congress programme, fall immeasurably below what is proposed as a condition of permanently attaching the colonies to England. The Indian nationalists do not seek parliamentary Government at home, and federation with England, they simply pray for the improvement and expansion of their legislative councils by the addition of a few representative members selected on the elective principle.

It is clear, again, that the Professor's idea of a nationality in India is that of the Hindu revivalists. It has been shown that the present national growth is not of that type, and that a revival of that sort is impossible under the present conditions. That the infantile growth now observable in India is of a kind which includes Hindus, Musulmans, Christians, and other races of India. Is there anything in the nature of things that would prevent the scheme of Government which the Professor proposes for the colonies, as the means of securing their permanent connection with the mother country, from being extended to India when the time comes? Of course that time is yet very, very remote; for to weld into a *common people* all the races of India, cannot be the work of a day, or even a century. But when this common people is fully formed, there will be a considerable portion of it who will claim distinct kindred with English people at home, and otherwise fulfil all the conditions for being a people of one *common State*, as the Professor defines it. How can the Professor deny the same scheme of Government to them as he proposes for the colonies?

The world looks as if, sooner or later, it would come to be divided into a few great political divisions. Sooner or later it will be the interest of all smaller States to amalgamate with some mightier State, and to form a people with its people. Why should not India, therefore, feel it her interest to be tacked to this "Greater Britain?" What will India and the Indians gain by severing themselves from England, if the Indians come to have, in reality, what, even now, they have in theory,—all the rights of British subjects?

There is a greater chance of the colonists thinking of separating themselves from the mother country than of the Indians ever doing so; for, in them, whatever ties of kindred exist (and such ties did not prevent the United States from declaring their independence), they cannot be stronger than the tie of gratitude of a united Indian people, if England honestly assists, as she has been hitherto doing, in the growth of that people. In India, again, the sense of liberty must always be tempered by a feeling of subordination to superiors in age, intellect, and position—a feeling which is engendered by the Indian family system, and which we hope will always remain a trait in our national character.

But these are idle speculations. It is an article of belief of the Indian Nationalists, that the conditions under which alone a nationality in India is growing and will grow, are, primarily, a common Government, and that Government, a British Government; and, as a corollary to that belief, they hold that there would be an end of all such hope if, by some disaster, the connection of England and India were to cease.

A REPLY TO MY CRITICS: OR WHAT IS THE HINDU RELIGION?

In the course of three articles which appeared in the *Calcutta Review* during the year 1890, and which were subsequently collected and published as a pamphlet, under the title of "An Introduction to the Study of Hinduism," it was maintained—

1st—That Hinduism is not a religious organization;

2nd—That what the Hindus, or the major portion in a Hindu community, do, is Hinduism;

3rd—That Hindus are those people of India who belong to a hierarchy of caste;

4th—That this caste system modifies itself according to the spirit of the times and surrounding circumstances; and

5th—That there is nothing in this caste system which renders it a bar to the growth of Indian nationalism.

While these propositions have been favourably received in many quarters, they have in others evoked adverse criticism, which it is the object of the present article to answer, and in doing so to examine the broader question—What is the Hindu Religion?

I have been told that I have disparaged Hinduism by saying "that it is not and has never been a religious organization; that it is a pure social system." My object was neither to disparage, nor to praise; but to state a truth. Yet it may not be amiss to ask, how the statement of that truth disparages the Hindu system. If it does anything, it exalts Hinduism according to my humble thinking. Hindus oftentimes commit the error, in the heat of controversy, without seeing what they gain thereby, of likening their system to other systems of the world. Some of them have also, without examining our own system, or taking a lesson from existing facts, imbibed an occidental mode of thought, and they cannot get over certain ideas, not very broad, regarding religion, which they have learnt from the conceptions of the West. To them religion is objective and not subjective; it is not the real, living faith of individual man, but his nominal adherence to a set of beliefs alleged to be the common faith of a community. To some of them it, perhaps, implies a book for a guide, and a book which claims to reveal the words of God; and, when twitted by an opponent with the question what they have to appeal to, they say it is the *Vedas*, forgetting that, in thus placing the claims of these in opposition to the Koran, or the Bible, they make their own system as narrow as, if not narrower than, one of these, and dependent on proofs,—moral, intellectual and historical—for the verification of such claims; and, while the Vedas, admittedly do not, like either the Koran, or the Bible, offer salvation to mankind at large on condition of the acceptance of their truths, those who set up their claims, can at best only claim that they are the guide of a portion of mankind, the rest being excluded from their benefit according to some canons of interpretation. And, even with this portion of mankind, the Vedas are not the only guide, as the Koran, or Bible, would be for its followers, but are supplemented by other authoritative works, laying down the rules of a Hindu's life, and claiming his faith as much as the Vedas themselves. Again, while these latter works express the utmost reverence for the Vedas, as the inspired source on which they draw, they shelve the Vedas and make room for themselves, by saying that the Vedas, in their entirety, were good for the *satya* yoke, while they are the guide for the present age of feebleness. You come, by this excuse for their existence, from one work to another. Perhaps all this marks the history of the evolution, or devolution, of Hinduism. Perhaps it marks the period when outside ideas were incorporated, or a glaring departure was made. Anyhow, if it is not the reflection of popular beliefs, popular beliefs have come to be in accord with it, and the people—those who know the Vedas (a very small number) and those who do not know them (a very large number),

—while manifesting the utmost reverence for the Vedas, shelve their claim by saying that they are too good for weak people like themselves. Thus the existing facts in Hindu society are completely destructive of the position that the Vedas are the guide of the Hindus at the present day, as the Bible, or Koran, is of its followers.

The Vedic gods, the Vedic rituals with but few exceptions, are not the gods or the rituals of any portion of the Hindus. Unless one were to ignore the evolution or devolution of centuries and completely forget the present, it is difficult to see how it can be said that the Hinduism of the day is the religion of the Vedic past. "Revive the Vedas, throw out the excrustation of centuries, the prejudices superadded to the original structure, you have what you want,—a national religion for the Hindus and a religious organization with social rites perfect in their nature as they were at the date of the Vedas." This, however, is a very large order, and after all, it may not lead us to a very hopeful prospect; for, to say nothing of the fact that certain canons of interpretation of the Vedas and Vedic rituals, favoured by the claimants of Vedic revival, might not be easily acceptable, it by no means meets the present need of India, as it makes exclusiveness, to our humble thinking, somewhat more exclusive. And what prospect is there of the revival of the Vedas. Only the other day there was some talk regarding the establishment of a Vedic Col lege in Calcutta. After some general discussion—which, as is the case with all such discussions, especially in Bengal, happened to be pointless,—a gentleman present raised the questions: Who were to be the professors? Who were to be the students? What interpretation of the Vedas was the College to adopt? What portions of the Vedas were to be read? These were eminently practical questions, and no steps could be made in advance without first solving them. There was a miniature representation of all parties in the little assembly that had met—those who believe in a progressive state of Hindu society, and its capacity for adapting itself to surrounding circumstances; the reactionists who would resist, if they could, this adaptibility; and those who would revive the Vedas, as a counterpoise to current Hinduism, but with an object quite different from that of the reactionists.

The question, therefore, was a sort of test—a feeler whether there could be concerted action between these classes. All sides thought that they could meet here, as on a common ground, and agree to the establishment of a College. Perhaps it was not the intention of any one section to take in the other, as their leaving the most important questions unsolved—and with them, perhaps, future seeds of quarrels and divisions—might seem to indicate. But when the questions were thus forced on them, it seemed as if the reactionists would have the College, without the solution; and one of them proposed, as the only business for that meeting, the formation of a Sub-Committee to devise the ways and means. But seeing what turn things were taking, the gentleman who had originally proposed the questions, moved that they be referred to the Sub-Committee and be considered before the question of ways and means. He succeeded in carrying his motion; and, in the discussion which followed, it was quickly discerned that the unanimity, which had previously existed, as to the desirability of establishing a Vedic College, was more apparent than real. When, however, the questions were about to be carried, in the way in which sensible people who would contribute to a project of this kind at the present day would have them carried, something like a threat was thrown out, that no Brahmin, to whom alone the knowledge of the *Vedas* was confined* would impart it to a Sudra, and the project of the establishment of a Vedic College remained in abeyance pending a report of the projector,† whose claim to the benefit of Vedic knowledge is yet doubtful, whether a Pundit could be found who would impart the knowledge of the Vedas to students who are Sudras. So much for the Vedic revival, and

* With regard to *Sham Veda,* a Pundit told the audience that the last man who knew it imparted the knowledge to him (the speaker) alone, and he had since imparted the knowledge to his brother and another of his pupils.

† Since this was written, the country had to mourn the death of this worthy gentleman.

Hinduism of the day being a religious organisation based, or to be based, on the Vedas.

Those who would not ignore existing facts, contend that, while the Vedas are the Old Testament, the *Puranas* and *Smrities* are the New Testament of the Hindus. If this affirmation were to be made with reference to a very small portion of the Hindus—say, Brahmins and one or two other castes amongst the Hindus—the proposition, even thus limited, would not be correct; for the Puranas and Smrities—and add to them the Tantras—are not among them identical compositions, with different interpretations given to them by different sects, as in Christianity or Muhamadanism, but distinct compositions: one claiming to be as authoritative as the other, and sometimes one prevailing in some part of the country where the other has no authority; or sometimes a number of them dividing their authority in that smallest unit of space—the village, or in that smallest of organisations—the family.

In an Indian village community all are Hindus—from Brahmins to Chamars, Domes and Mehtars,—who are not Musalmans.

The mistake begins in at once jumping to the conclusion that it is religion, that is to say—religious faith—which divides these Hindus from the Musalmans. Yet I know personally of a case, where, amongst people who pass as Hindu, there is one who believes in the revelation of the Koran, in the *Kalma*, and repeats *Namajes* five times a day according to the orthodox Koran rituals. Amongst the Hindus not more than 15 per cent. of the population are in touch with the Brahmins, the rest are below that touch. If the Vedas were to be revived, a number, but not the whole, of this 15 per cent., will have a claim, according to accepted canons of exclusion and inclusion, to a knowledge of the Vedas, Vedic worship and Vedic rites; at present, however, excepting the followers of Dayanand Saraswati (not even a perceptible percentage), who pass under the name of Aryans, and who accept the Vedas as their only guide, under a canon of interpretation adopted by Pundit Dayanand, the rest of the 15 per cent. have not much to do *directly* with Vedic worship, or Vedic rituals; and so far as what my friends call the New Testament, the *Puranas*, the *Smrities*, and *Tantras*, each and all, as we said, have their authority over divisions and sub-divisions in detail, so that, while the utmost diversity of religious faith prevails in this upper 15 per cent., it is hard to say that the religious faith of a particular individual of the community resembles, in all respects, that of his neighbour.

Of the remaining 85 per cent., though a considerable portion in Bengal are the followers of Vaisnav Gosains, he would be a bold man who should say that theirs is the religion of the Vedas, of any particular Puran, or of any known kind of Tantra. It is always changing, and it changes in a way unknown

phlet was written and published. There is a great and striking similarity in thought, and even in expressions, which,—if to others who do not know the fact, it might seem to show that I have borrowed largely from the Professor's book without any acknowledgment—shows to me, that we can only arrive at the same truth by independent enquiry of our own, and that the expression of that truth would be in almost the same words; but though the premises are the same, and expressed almost in the same words, the conclusion differs. My conclusion from certain facts is, that though the Hindu is intensely religious, Hinduism (possibly because of that intense religiousness), is not a religious organization. The Professor finds nothing common in India, with its diverse races, diverse languages, diverse social customs and manners, and diversity of caste, but a common religion—a common faith;—I showed that Hinduism is not simply a social organization, but that what the Hindus, or the majority of Hindus in a Hindu community *do*, is Hinduism; that to be a Hindu, or to continue a Hindu, one must belong to a hierarchy of caste. That the caste hierarchy, which involves an admission, even at the present day, of the supremacy of the Brahmins, does not involve, or imply, a religious faith in such supremacy, any more than the admission of an aristocracy, either of birth or of wealth, would do in cases where such distinctions prevail.

In treating of modern castes (p. 157) the Professor

says: "It might almost, indeed, be inferred from the influence exerted by caste rules on the daily life of the Hindus, that the whole of their religion was centered in caste observances, and that Hinduism and caste were convertible terms, and, in point of fact, strictness in the maintenance of caste is the only test of Hinduism exacted by the Brahmins of the present day. In matters of mere faith, Hinduism is (as we have seen) all tolerant and receptive: no person, who is not born a Brahmin, can become one, but any person can be admitted in the lower ranks of Hinduism, who will acknowledge the supremacy of the Brahmins and obey the rules of caste. So long as a man holds to his caste, he is at liberty to hold any opinions he likes, even to accepting the doctrines of Christianity.

'Perfection is alone attained by him who swerves not from the business of his caste.'"—*(Bhagwatgita.)*

I ask whether from the above premise—in which, however, we detect one or two statements not in accord with the present rules of caste, for instance, the reference to the great strictness with which rules of caste are said to be enforced by the *Brahmins* (the fact being that it is not the Brahmins, but caste-people, who enforce the rules), but which does not affect the correctness of the premise in the main—it does not follow, as I have said, that Hinduism is not a religious organization, but a social organization, pure and simple, and whether this does not fully corroborate what I stated in my pamphlet.

to be classed in this way, and the people of Kuch Behar, who were, under the ruling of the Bengal Census Commissioner, to be classed as Kuchis, or Kuch Beharies, are to be classed as Hindus, in accordance with their application in that behalf; the other non-Aryan Hill-tribes have also successfully preferred their claims to be classed as Hindus.

It must be a matter of agreeable surprise to all Hindus, that, though they do not spend a pice for evangelization, there is such a scrambling among all classes of people in Hindustan, excepting, of course, the Christians, Mahomedans and Parsis, to be recognized as Hindus, and when a better understanding comes on, we hope we shall have Hindus-Christians; and Hindus-Mahomedans.

But the returns under column "sect," of the Hindus will be even at present an interesting study, and in a greater degree illustrative of our position. A large class of men in Behar, and people elsewhere have been returned as Bhagwats. Primarily the word means भक्त (Sanskrit) *devoted*, secondarily the भक्त of Srimat Bhagwat; but in Behar and elsewhere in Northern India, the word has lost both its primary and secondary meanings, and it now means "people who abstain from spirituous liquors of all sorts, meat and fish." The word thus includes not only Vaisnavs, but all the Nanakpanthi followers of the early Guru Nanak, who abstain from fish, meat and spirituous liquors—according to his teachings, a very large number among the lower classes of Behar, as also some amongst the higher classes,—a large number of Kabirpanthis, and other nondescripts, such as one or two converts to Hinduism from Mahomedanism, to our certain knowledge.

We shall have to examine the late census proceedings in connection with another position we referred to wherein, in showing the elasticity of caste rules, we observed that there is a general attempt at upheaval amongst the masses.

Now, we have Hindu-Jains, Hindu-Sikhs, Hindu-Nanak-Sahes, Hindu-Kabirpanthis, Hindu-Brahmos, Hindu-Sophists, Hindu-Agoris, Hindu-Positivists, Hindu-Ghonds, Hindu-Bhils, Hindu-Sonthals, as well as Hindu-Vedics and Hindu-Puranicks. There is not the slightest obstacle, so far as faith is concerned, to our having Hindu-Christians and Hindu-Musalmans, and, as I showed above, we have even now some such amongst us.

The *Vedas* give evidence of a progressive religion. The *Maha-Nirvan Tantra*, one of the latest phases of religious systems in India, leaves room for any amount of addition to the *Agam* and *Nigam*. Moreover, it introduces into the system the doctrine of सिद्धपुरुष (inspired men), and, if outsiders have to teach us anything new in the domain of religion let them give it to us as trutns brought home to them by a सिद्धपुरुष.

It follows that the definition of this Hindu religion, which has already absorbed so many systems, and

It is one of these eldest sons of India who said:—

अधिकारिणिभेदेन पश्य वाङ्कल्यतः प्रिये ।
देवा नानाविधाः प्रोक्ता देत्योह्यपि वङ्कधा प्रिये ॥
महानिर्व्वाण तन्त्र ।

"There are different Gods and Goddesses, my beloved, according to the varying stages of development of the *adhikari* (owner)."

And another said in consequence:—

ये यथा मां प्रपद्यन्ते तां तथो भज्यम्यहं ।
भागवतगीता ।

"In whatever form a man may worship me, I accept it in that form."

One said:—

चिन्मयस्याद्वितीयस्य निष्कलस्याशरीरिणः
उपासकानां कार्य्यार्थं ब्रह्मणो रूपकल्पना ॥
रूप स्थानां देवतानां पुं स्त्र्यांशादिकल्पना ।
स्मार्त्तधृत यमदग्नि वचन

"The devotee, for the purpose of devotion, imagines to himself a form of the Deity who is without form, without a denomination, without a second, and is all-wise. When imagination is allowed play, the form imagined is that of man or of woman."

And another said:—

रूप नानादिनिर्द्देशविशेषणविवर्ज्जितः
अपक्षयविनाशाभ्यां परिणामर्त्ति जन्मभिः
वर्जितः शक्यते वक्तुं यः सदास्तीति केवलम् ।
विष्णु पुराण ।

"The supreme soul is without the attribute of form or name, indestructible, and not subject to pain or birth. The only thing that can be predicated of Him is, that *He exists*."

It is remarkable that the term Hindu now invariably adopted by all classes of people inhabiting India, as applicable to themselves, with the exception of Musalmans, Christians, and Parsis, are not to be found in any Sanscrit books pretending to any antiquity. There are some people (followers of Dyanand Saraswati), a small number, who say that, because the name is of foreign origin and latterly applied by Musalmans as a term of opprobrium to the natives of the country, the name should be discarded, and the name Aryan adopted instead. Some of the Brahmos, too, of the Sadharan Brahma Samaj, by birth Hindus, evincc something like horror at being called Hindus. It is to be hoped that they will ennoble by their life-examples the new names which they have adopted; but to the Dyanandi Aryans we say, the best way to rid a national name of its opprobrium is to stick to it, and to ennoble it by the life-example of those bearing the common name, and not by flying from one name to another. The Thebans, the Bœotians of the Greeks, even now a nick-name, stuck to their name and became, when the glory of Spartans and Athenians had fled, the most prominent race amongst the Greeks. Does the name serve to explain in any way the position we started? I suppose it does. And that is why I advert to it. And, in this connection, we shall examine the origin of the term, under what circumstances the Hindus adopted it, and what it means at the present date.

It is just possible that the dwellers on the banks of the Indus and its tributaries, both Aryans and non-Aryans, were called by the people living more to the West, *Sindhus*, and they themselves passed by that name, as an appropriate geographical denomination of themselves. The Persians and their neighbours of the West pronounced *Sindhus*, Hindus, as latterly the Greeks, dropping the hard aspirate, called the Persian word Hindu "Indu" and the country they inhabited "India." The Persians calling the country "Hindustan" from the Punjab to Benares, the Musalmans extended the name first to all the country north of the Vindhya chain and then to the whole country from the Indus to the Brahmaputra and from the Himalaya to Cape Comorin. Not that a common geographical name had not been given by the people of the pre-Mahomedan period to the country at large, though it was divided into several states *Bharat* was such a name, and *Arya Barta* such another; and the conquering race called themselves *Aryans*, just as another conquering race in another country called themselves Franks, and the aborigines *Dasas or Dasyas* (robbers), *Krishna Varna* (black colour) and latterly *non-Aryans* (अनार्य्य). There must have been very sharp lines of distinction between the Aryans and non-Aryans at one time. The Aryans worshipped their own gods, the non-Aryans theirs. The non-Aryans lived beyond the out-skirts of Aryan settlements, and those who lived within were reduced to slavery, as the condition on which they were allowed to exist. Gradually, as time wore on, things mended a good deal. The Aryan influence extended not only by conquest and colonization, but also by conversion, marriages, and political alliances. With the acclimatization of the Aryans, they adopted some of the non-Aryan customs and manners, and introduced some of their gods into their Pantheon. The non-Aryans did the same; but, as the *Vedas* were in a language known only to the Aryans, they had no means of attaining to a knowledge of the *Vedas*, which, afterwards, by a process of exclusiveness, was confined to the Aryan class, or such of the non-Aryans as the Dravidan races, which by treaty alliances came to be held to be equal to the Aryans. The distinction engendered, of the inequality of conquerors and conquered, of *Aryans* and *Dasyas*, of white and black, of masters and slaves, and of the whites amongst themselves, on account of differences of knowledge, prowess, position and occupation gave place to caste distinctions, which began to grow, and with them fictions of a common origin from the same *Brahma*, or from the same *Manu*, but for different purposes. This, perhaps, was the earliest enunciation of an identity of race, vague and indistinct. At last, common danger from external foes, which overwhelmed the Aryans and non-Aryans alike, gave rise to a community of feelings and sentiments; and it was at this stage, it appears, that the common *Hindu* name was adopted, in the sense of a people all of the same country, 'Hindustan,' as opposed to the foreigners—Musalman invaders. It was not, as can be gathered from this historic origin, the name of a people having a common religion, but a people who adopted this common name, as a bond of union among themselves, to avoid a common danger and to repel a common foe. This common name indicative of complex ideas—geographical, social, racial, political—originated in the same way as a common national life has grown in any other geographical division. Mr. Mill, in his exposition of nationality, says:—

"A portion of mankind may be said to constitute a nationality, if they are united amongst themselves, by common sympathies, which do not exist between them and any others, which make them co-operate with each other more willingly than with other people, and desire to be under the same Government by themselves, or a portion of themselves, exclusively. This feeling of nationality may have been generated by various causes. Sometimes it is the effect of identity of race and descent. Community of language, and community of religion, greatly contribute to it.

"Geographical limits are one of its causes. But

the *strongest of all* is identity of political antecedents, the possession of a national history, and consequent community of recollections; collective pride and humiliation, pleasure and regret, connected with the same incidents in the past. None of these circumstances, however, are either indispensible or necessarily sufficient by themselves."

The Aryans and non-Aryans of India forgot their differences and adopted a common name, which the Persians had given to them, in token of their common sympathy in view of a common danger, and co-operated with each other, however temporarily and however unsuccessfully, to keep up the Government of their own, or a portion of their own. Their humiliations, their regrets, connected with their failure, as also the traditionary pleasant reminiscences of the past to which Aryans and non-Aryans now equally laid claim as a people, however varying the religious idea amongst them—made them one. It is thus found that the term '*Hindu*' originally signified a geographical *Hindu*, that is people living in the same country; then the idea became more complex, and signified a national or political '*Hindu*,' as applied by the Aryans and non-Aryans of India to themselves, distinguishing themselves from their foreign invaders; and at that date *Hinduism* was a political and not a religious organization.

But a critic asks, what is my object in thus trying to make out that Hinduism is not a religious organization. I say to my critic that my object is simply to state a truth; but if he wishes to know what is the value of that truth, he, at least, I hope, will bear with me in the little digression that follows:—We have pointed out that the idea involved in the term was originally geographical; it afterwards came to be political, and it had nothing special of religion about it, except that it differentiated the class thus designated from the Mahomedans, who, out of contempt, called their foes—Aryans and non-Aryans, the wise *Brahmins* and the ignorant *Bhils*—*Kafirs*, that is to say non-believers in a revealed book. Thus, even in the inception, so far as the *religious element* was concerned, a kind of negation came to be associated with the idea. The idea of a nationality in this sense came to be developed, when the Hindu-Sikhs rose to be a nation. This idea which was prominently before those who had the forming of the Sikhs into a nation, could but include a portion of the then existing people of the Punjab, and their circumstances required that it should be such. This was the weakest point, and the growth was not at all healthy, but it succeeded to a certain extent, because it had effectually united the Aryans and non-Aryans in a common political body. Even the *Mehtars* (sweepers of the Hindus, the lowest of the low) had their position in the political body. They were formed into regiments, and had the term '*Sinha*' applied to them, like other Sikhs.

The growth of the Mahratta power, the rise of another branch of the Hindu race, demonstrates the same position. In so far as it produced a solidarity amongst the Aryans and non-Aryans of a portion of India, it grew. The *Kambis*, the *Gaekwars*, and so on—classes otherwise despised by Brahmins—came to have a recognized position, and the identity of aim made all co-operate in the same direction. Community of religion did not play much part in the fostering of that growth. All the Aryans and non-Aryans became politically developed Hindus, because it was their interest to be so,—but the weakness was latent. Both these movements were directed against an important section of the population of the country, which could not be effaced, and the result was partial growth and eventual collapse.

To avert common danger from foreign invasions, the *Aryans* and *non-Aryans* coalesced under the common name *Hindu;* is it too much to expect that all the people of India will again coalesce under a common name, and this time avoid the errors of the past? The Hindus became a prey to foreigners, because, though they became one in name, it was at a very late hour of the day, when there was no time for solidarity, and afterwards, the idea, as it was at first associated with the name, became out of date, or capable only of partial development, as we find in the growth of the powers of the *Mahrattas* and the *Sikhs*.

Let not the error be repeated. It lies with the existing Government, as well as with the people, to avoid the mistake. True statesmanship, while assisting in the growth of this highest '*Indianism*,' as securing the ultimate good of a vast portion of mankind, ought to avoid anything calculated to produce the least friction between party and party. The people, on the other hand, ought to understand and fully realize the truth, which is apparent, that it is not possible in the nature of things that any one of the existing sections of the population shall be effaced. There may now be apparent conflicts—there may be at times outbursts of fanatical intolerance, but there is much evaporation in our sunny clime of Ind. A critic was good enough to point out to me that *Islam* is as intolerant as ever, and the spirit of reaction is growing in European Turkey and Europeanised Persia, and in these days of rapid communication, by the aid of steamers, telegrams and newspaper, the reactionary move is coming on *apace* in India. I read in the *Contemporary Review* of February last, an interesting article on the subject of this reaction and its causes, by one of the highest authority on the subject, Prince Malcolm Khan. He says that this reaction is simply the expression of the resentment of *Islam* against the intrusiveness, or supposed intrusiveness of Christianity. To use his own words "the whole history of Asia Minor has been one long fight with Christianity. They (the Persians) know well the history of the Crusades, and they think that your present policy is still a crusade, but only in a more civilized form. A crusade of science. It is still the Christian religion, which attacks Islamism, but instead of attacking it, as in past times, by arms, it attacks it by science, by policy, by trade, and by financial power. But the situation is just the same. Under these circumstances anything coming from Europe is opposed and must be opposed." Wherever really there is no such intrusiveness, wherever there is a brotherly welcome, as in India,* the intolerance if any, supposed without examination of the grounds thereof, to be inherent in *Islamism*, gives way, and a factious and *fictitious* reactionary move, even if stimulated by extraneous influences, soon disappears.

We showed, in a previous article, how this supposed intolerance gave way in India, and how all reactionary moves amongst our Mahomedan brethren in relation to Hinduism have been only temporary. In this connection we shall ask the curious reader to read further a few chapters of the early life of *Chaitanya*, his relation with the Mahomedan *Kazi* of Navadip, and the *Kirtan* (singing procession) near about the *Kazi's* house. The conversion of Rup Sanatan, the life of Kabir, the life of Nanak, and the life of many

* The Hindu ascetic who used to be carried up by a ladder and placed on a platform separate from the room where Akbar used to sit for his evening discussions, so as to avoid the touch of the Royal Melecha, yet taught him the high doctrine of toleration to all religious views.

Mahomedans, Aooelia Sophies of the present day, whose religious teachings sway the inner life of most of our Mahomedan brethren. But the further question is: "Is the spirit of Islam antagonistic to progress?"

Let us hear what Prince Malcolm has to say—(it may, perhaps, remind our readers, of what we said of Hinduism in April last year):—

"Islam, as I have said, is an ocean, in which are accumulated all the sciences of the past times of Asia —then for any new law or new principle you wish to promulgate, you can find in that ocean many precepts and maxims which support and confirm what you want to introduce. As to the principles which are found in Europe, which constitute the root of your civilization, we must get hold of them, somehow no doubt, but, instead of taking them from London or Paris, it would be easy to take the same principle and to say it comes from Islam, and that this can be soon proved. We have had some experience in this direction. We find that ideas which were by no means accepted when coming from your agents in Europe, were accepted at once with the greatest delight when it was proved that they were latent in Islam. I can assure you that the little progress which we see in Persia and Turkey, specially in Persia, is due to this fact, that some people have taken your European principles, and, instead of saying that they came from Europe, from England, France, or Germany, have said

—'We have nothing to do with Europeans; these are the true principles of our own religion (and, indeed, that is quite true), which have been taken by Europeans.' that has had a marvellous effect at once."

A disregard of a like sensitiveness as regards extraneous influences by Government, and by people who wish to introduce reforms amongst the Hindus and Mahomedans in India, has been fruitful of mistakes, resulting in temporary reaction and arrest of progress.

So far as the Hindus are concerned, sometimes a reaction originating in an error (a common one) that to move the masses, to produce "a national life" in India, religion must come in, and a religion common to all Hindus, has retarded progress. To move the masses and to produce a national life, are not, however always convertible terms; and then, what is this common religion which the good-meaning people intend to give us? It cannot, if what we have said in the preceding pages is correct, be the *Sanatan Hindu Dharma.* The keynotes of that *Sanatan Dharma* are harmonious to religious feelings in man, and their expression is always varied and varying.

We have said that Hinduism represents a progressive state of religious knowledge and faith, and that it is in these respects eclectic. We shall now show that so far as the *Karmas*—works (rituals and ceremonies)—are concerned it is eclectic also. A few words of preface appear necessary. We showed, in a

as Hindus, have fallen back more or less on these written codes, and the interpretation thereof by the Pundits,* the lower classes have still to depend on their *Punchait*, to declare what the unwritten law is, and the kind of sanction for its non-observance. Nowhere is this *Punchait* system found in a more developed form than among the lower orders of the people of Behar: among the classes of Kairis, Kurmis, Kahars, Telis, &c. We find among them five grades of caste councils: Gawan, Jawar, Baisi, Panchmahal, and Chaurasi; of which the first is the lowest court, and the last the highest court of appeal. An ap-

* The principal centres of these Pundits in Bengal are Navadip, Tribini, Vicrampur and Backla. The Pundits are either mere grammarians, (Vyakaranik), lawyers (Smartas), or logicians (Nyaeks). The Nyaeks hold the highest rank; next to the Nyaeks are the Smartas, and last comes the Vyakaranik. The Bengal Nyaeks obtain their title in the *toles*, by reading the Nya-shastra (logic). The curriculum does not include any system of Darshan (philosophy), or any of the Vedas or Puranas, or Dharma Shastra (law). The Smartas read only the Dharma Shastras prevalent in the Bengal School—Dyabhaga and Raghunandan's compilation of Smrities. The Vyakaraniks obtain their title on account of proficiency in grammar and rhetoric. The Pundits subsist on alms. For reasons very similar to those which influenced our courts to disregard the Vyvasthas of the Court Pundit, when the Court Pundit was an institution in our courts, the Samajiks disregard their Vyvasthas in many cases. In all parts of India the Pundits have to give Vyvasthas only in cases when the matter is referred to them by the caste-people.

peal cannot go direct to the Chaurasi, but must pass through the intermediate courts. The Gawan Council consists of members chosen from two or more conterminous villages. The word Jawar literally means 'neighbour,' but in this case signifies a tract of country composed of villages surrounding the family residence of some recognized person. Its extent is fixed; but, of course, there can be no rule regulating the number of villages which make up a Jawar. The term Baisi signifies a court consisting of 22 *Punchaits*, but this number is not strictly adhered to. The *Panchmahal* has a still larger jurisdiction; and the *Chaurasi* is the supreme over all, its jurisdiction extending over several districts.

Every *Punchait* has a Sardar, or headman, called *Mahtan*, whose office is hereditary. But, should the son be incompetent, the members of the caste proceed to elect another headman; and the office remains in the new family, except in the case above alluded to, or on failure of male issue. Offences triable by *Punchaits* may be broadly classified thus:—(1) Civil claims, (2) Social offences in which the women of the family are concerned, and where exposure would be disgraceful, (3) Assault, abusive language, &c., (4) Theft, (5) Extortion, (6) 'Maintenance.' The punishments are fine and social ostracism. An aggrieved party first goes to the Sardar and makes his complaint. If he has a *primâ facie* case, the Chhari Sardar (Chaprasi) of the *Punchaits* is sent to suming our fight from your serene and august distance, and exercising your right of dissolving our Paddington Parliaments as often as you see that we do not rise to the height of telling our countrymen; 'Practise not that which is legal under your sacred ordinances, but is abhorred by the world at large, (for) it secures not celestial bliss,' and sanctioning our decrees in your Supreme Council when we do. This at least will save you from the pain of having your benevolent motives misconstrued and misunderstood.

To one section of my countrymen I say, we are moving, however imperceptibly, by ourselves; and it is not easy to move a whole nation, and the life of a nation is, at any rate, very long indeed. We cannot be moved by extraneous forces, for the whole social fabric is so framed that, if you apply extraneous force at one part, there is a danger of the whole coming to a dead-lock at another part. And if it ought not to touch our *amour propre* to be told to move by a legislature composed almost entirely of foreigners, we know that they do not understand us, our social system and our difficulties. Consider the above premises, when you seek extraneous aid, and if you wish us to move faster than we are doing at present, the first thing you should do, is to apply your head and heart to get some sort of voice in the Legislative Councils of India, or at best to get revived the Councils indicated in the "Mitakshara," as Councils subordinate to the Supreme Councils, where you and your countrymen alone should decide what is for the good of your own social well-being.

To another section of my countrymen, I say: Under no mood forget that the *Sonatan Hindu Dhàrma* is a moving and progressive system, and, so far as its social ethics are concerned, it is settled by the voice of people, or say a majority of people, with regard to surrounding circumstances as to their ultimate good. The expression of that voice differs from time to time as the changing circumstances differ, and there is a relativity, as in other ideas, in our idea of the ultimate good of our people. You have made your customs, and you make your customs even now, by adherence to the above premises, and while you should never cease to join with the rest of your countrymen in trying to achieve some amount of political freedom by getting a voice in your Legislative Councils, see that, with the limited and narrow powers you even now possess, you conform so well to the true spirit of your system, to the true spirit of the times, and to the surrounding circumstances that you give not even the slightest excuse for any extraneous forces being ever brought to bear on you.

To all my countrymen I say: Join hands and proceed on your onward march.